C000070408

SCANDAL
ANNUAL
1990

The Paragon Project

SCANDAL

ANNUAL

1990

Who Got Caught Doing What in 1989

ST. MARTIN'S PRESS   NEW YORK

ISBN 0-312-03928-X

First Edition

10 9 8 7 6 5 4 3 2 1

To Nancy and Ryan T., for being paragons

CONTENTS

INTRODUCTION

Welcome to the fourth edition of *Scandal Annual*, the yearly chronicle of the misdoings and misdeeds of the famous, infamous and, possibly, your friends and neighbors.

The year 1989 was a banner year for all kinds of scandals. As in recent years, political scandals captured major headlines. For example, in 1989 we learned that the top officials of HUD spent eight years giving an entirely new meaning to the words *house sale*. Over on Capitol Hill, the latest synonym for *congressman* became *defendant*. In the Executive Branch, Dan Quayle's primary responsibility as Vice President seemed to be accumulating enough gaffes to fill a one-man celebrity-bloopers show.

In the world of sex, the top story was Rob Lowe's racy new video, *Two Men and a Baby*. Among the most sensational divorces of the year were Madonna and Sean Penn's (amid reports that Penn tied Madonna to a chair and left her for eight hours) and Robin Givens and Mike Tyson's (amid reports that she was his favorite sparing partner). The most incredible report came from across the ocean, where it was revealed that the decidedly matronly Princess Anne wrote a series of steamy scarlet letters.

Greed also made lots of headlines this year, topped by the astoundingly tacky, vicious antics of Leona Helmsley. An unauthorized bio of the famous Jackie Onassis toppled her and the very randy President John F. Kennedy from their pedestals, while baseball immortal Pete Rose was slugged with serious charges of very mortal sins that resulted in a lifetime ban from baseball.

As usual, actors, actresses, authors, and other celebrities contributed dozens of juicy scandals too numerous to mention here. For the convenience of our readers, we've organized these scandals into a special celebrity "Sin-dex" so you can find out if your favorite star made the headlines this year. We've collected hundreds of funny, sad, and bizarre scandals involving the vast majority of people whose names aren't household words. *Scandal Annual 1990: Who Got Caught Doing What in 1989* contains stories about the most brazen, the greediest, the dumbest, and the just plain unluckiest people of 1989. Enjoy.

SCANDAL
ANNUAL
1990

1

SCANDALOUS
QUOTES OF 1989

At first, he was closely related to Sir John Macdonald, the first prime minister of Canada. The moment he was disqualified, he came from Jamaica.

> —John Candy, on disgraced Canadian
> sprinter Ben Johnson

I never beat up women. I only beat them up with $100 bills, diamonds, and mink coats.

> —Mike Tyson, defending himself

That's the Who.

> —Ron Wood, Rolling Stones guitarist,
> when asked if his band was touring
> for the money

Sometimes I think that if it weren't for show business, many of us would be in the streets carrying signs that say, "The End of the World Is Coming."
> —Carrie Fisher, on the mental stability of celebrities

GREAT MOMENTS IN LOGIC

It's really hard to maintain a one-on-one relationship if the other person is not going to allow me to be with other people.
> —Axl Rose, Guns 'n' Roses singer

I need them for distances, even though I think with some of the mistakes I've made in life, I could have used them for close-up endeavors, too.
> —Sylvester Stallone, on his new glasses

Maybe it's a little understated.
> —Corporate financier Saul Steinberg, describing a lavish birthday party that featured live nude models posing as famous Flemish paintings

Matt Dillon's underwear.
> —Boy George, when asked what he wanted to be reincarnated as

I know Don Johnson and he is scum. He's just a long-haired guy with good looks who makes a bundle selling sex, drugs, and violence on commercial television.
> —Senator Jay Rockefeller of West Virginia

IN THE UNREPENTANT SINNER DEPARTMENT

I'd like to see people, instead of spending so much time on the ethical problem, get after the problems that really affect the people of this country.
>   —Richard Nixon

INFAMOUS LAST WORDS

We forgot to discuss the dating habits of our flight attendants so we could get it on the recorder before we crashed. Then the media would have some kind of a juicy tidbit.
>   —Joke tape-recorded by a Delta cockpit
>   crew member—a few minutes before
>   his flight really *did* crash

At school, they asked him what his dad does for a living, and he said, "He sleeps in a trailer."
>   —Actor Michael Keaton, on his 6-year-
>   old son's impression of visiting his
>   father on the set of *Batman*

HOLLYWOOD

There are wonderfully talented young people, and then you meet the scum of the earth. I wouldn't want my kids near them. I've worked for some of them. They're in the bushes and under rocks.
>   —John Candy on Hollywood

Never. The cops are afraid of me. Plus, I send them $20,000 a year just to leave me alone.
>   —Sandra Bernhard, when asked if she
>   ever was stopped by police

Nobody's going to pay $15 million to have sex. It may get some little bit-part actress a $400 role if they're up for a part in, like, *Babe's in Bimboland.*

> —Kirstie Alley, dispelling the myth of
> the casting couch

You know you are overdoing it when you fall over. But it was easy to stop. Just a desire not to bump my head anymore, I guess.

> —Mel Gibson, on why he cut down on
> his drinking

IN THE FRIGHTENING THOUGHTS DEPARTMENT

We are your parents' worst nightmare . . . because we are your parents.

> —Rock singer Grace Slick, upon turning
> 50

If you want anything said, ask a man. If you want anything done, ask a woman.

> —British Prime Minister Margaret
> Thatcher

The only time I got depressed about aging was on my 27th birthday, because I saw that as the end of real youth.

> —Joan Collins, on an event from her
> distant past

What's happening in music today is very corrupting. Let's help our children toss out the garbage.

> —What Bruce Springsteen did not say
> about modern music. The erroneous
> quote, which appeared in *Reader's
> Digest,* was used in the latest
> propaganda film produced by the
> Parents' Music Resource Center. The
> Boss was allegedly furious.

I never got into fights with kids about whose dad is bigger and who can beat up who. What am I going to say? My dad can kill your dad when he's asleep?
> —Michael Brunner, son of Charles Manson

Yes, a thirty-minute delivery is important, but safe delivery is more important.
> —Domino Pizza President Dave Black, after numerous reports that reckless driving by pizza deliverers had resulted in several accidents

On the back page was a listing of National League cities. New York, Chicago, Cincinnati, St. Louis. And next to each city there was a woman's name and phone number. Some of the names had stars next to them. It was horrible. Too horrible.
> —Cyndy Garvey, on opening her ex-husband Steve's appointment book

All the people I have in my office, they can't speak English properly, they can't write properly. All the letters sent from my office I have to correct myself, and that is because English is taught so bloody badly.
> —Prince Charles, lamenting the state of British education

Dating is more stressful than prison.
> —Cathy Evelyn Smith, on her incarceration for injecting actor John Belushi with a fatal dose of drugs

We have plans to develop this into a modern shooting complex for both the public and the Army. Shooting and knowing how to shoot is just part of being Nicaraguan.
> —Manager of a gun range in Managua

I'd have Dan Rather read the news in a chair attached to a dunk tank. There'd be an 800 number for viewers to try calling, and the right random combinations of digits would drop him in the water.

> —Steve O'Donnell, head writer for
> David Letterman, on his thoughts for
> boosting TV news ratings

I had no idea that you had fallen so far. Do they pay you well?

> —Walter Cronkite to former newsman
> Bill Boggs, when he found out Boggs
> was executive producer of the now
> defunct "Morton Downey, Jr., Show"

She showed me how to put the hand in the pocket with your index finger and flip-flop your hand.

> —Rich Little, describing how Barbara
> Bush had helped him work on his
> impression of her husband

I'm very stunned and flattered and glad to learn that the rest of Mr. Will's body is not as conservative as his brain.

> —Susan Sarandon, when told that she
> made George Will's list of what he'd
> like to take to another planet

I haven't lost weight, didn't wear drag, and nobody broke my nose. But the Queen still recognized me.

> —ABC radio talk-show host Michael
> Jackson, on being honored by
> Britain's Queen Elizabeth

Now when I go back to Texas, I see the same guys who used to beat me up, walking around in sweat-stained T-shirts with big beer bellies. You know what I mean?

> —Movie star Patrick Swayze, on the best
> revenge

From my mother's life I knew what I didn't want: to be a product, an image, and in real life, nothing.

—Tahnee Welch, on her mother Raquel

She says things like, "Uh, what did you think about my last phone call?"

—Gossip columnist Liz Smith, on Raquel Welch

I'll call my mother and say, "You're going to read that I just got married, but believe me, I would have invited you."

—Singer Sheena Easton, on tabloid gossip

I think the sexiest thing a woman could do is be as fat as me—or fatter.

—Roseanne Barr

I don't know what kind of doctor I am, but watching all these sisters . . . I'm debating whether I should be a gynecologist.

—Mike Tyson, receiving an honorary degree from Central State University in Ohio

Forget about Rambo. Mark is double the size. I mean everywhere. We are dealing with a Viking here. Extra, extra, extra large.

—Brigitte Nielsen, comparing ex-hubby Sylvester Stallone to lover Mark Gastineau

She's one of the most sexually experienced women I have ever met, by the way, and I respect that. I love her a helluva lot more than football.

—Mark Gastineau, on Brigitte Nielsen

Hey, listen, I'm a member of the NRA. You're hurting my feelings, as they say in China.

> —George Bush, after he was asked why he didn't condemn violence against women while addressing the National Rifle Association

The hors d'oeuvres would have been better, but none of us do any HUD work.

> —A Republican, about a party celebrating a court decision that overturned Lyn Nofziger's conviction for illegal lobbying

In all fairness, there were others who didn't get along with him. He's a very difficult man to work for.

> —An FBI agent, commenting on a boss who survived an employee's attempt to kill him by putting cyanide in the water cooler

I loved the danger. He was so exciting. I can't describe it. He was a turn-on. I think what people don't realize with a certain type of woman, that there are times when she wants the man she's with to be . . . a man.

> —Robin Givens, on Mike Tyson

We wouldn't make a sequel, but we may well make a second episode.

> —Jon Peters, producer of *Batman*

Nice to have you here on such a historic night.

> —Host of a cable TV home-shopping show on which Pete Rose appeared to hawk souvenirs on the night he was suspended from baseball

Kinda weird, kinda me, kinda strange—kinda like Disneyland on acid—and I'm the E ticket, okay?
> —Cher, on her stage show

If I had a choice of having a woman in my arms or shooting a bad guy on a horse, I'd take the horse. It's a lot more fun.
> —Heartthrob Kevin Costner

I used to eat while I was in the supermarket. I guess I didn't consider it stealing 'cause I took it out inside my body.
> —Comedian and talk-show host Arsenio Hall

A LITERARY EXCHANGE

In my mind, there is something silly about a man who wears a white suit all the time, especially in New York.
> —Norman Mailer, on Tom Wolfe

The lead dog is the one they always try to bite in the ass.
> —Tom Wolfe, replying to Mailer

It doesn't mean you're top dog just because your ass is bleeding.
> —The last word, from Norman Mailer

It was a good experience until I realized she had a need to say the word *penis* more than 111,000 times in a six-minute interview.
> —Comedian Richard Lewis, on Dr. Ruth Westheimer's show

I hope your family dies in a plane crash.
> —Presidential son Michael Reagan, concluding a profanity-riddled message he left on the answering machine of a photographer who sued Reagan for copyright infringement

We have both dressed in green.
>—Nicaraguan President Daniel Ortega,
>summing up the areas of agreement
>after his meeting with British Prime
>Minister Margaret Thatcher

A friend of mine who wears wings told me, "I would never fly it. You'd never jump out of a plane that cost $600 million."
>—Former Pentagon official Robert
>Costello, on the Stealth bomber

I'd like to work my way down to two chins, thank you. Then I'll have one of those liposuction deals with a canister vacuum.
>—"Roseanne" star John Goodman

WHATEVER YOU DO, KEEP IT OFF YOUR WALLET

Wear it anywhere you want to be touched.
>—Elizabeth Taylor, on her new perfume
>for men

I think I single-handedly put the girdle industry out of business—now I'd like to bring it back.
>—Lauren Hutton, on being 45 years old

They're scum. I just don't understand why we subsidize people who just go on holiday all the time.
>—Elvis Costello, on Britain's royal
>family

We were aware something was about to happen, but we did not know what.

> —Fortune-teller Margaret Pickering, on premonitions felt by a group of psychics just before all of their crystal balls and tarot cards were stolen

To boldly go where no rock 'n' roll band's gone before, to search out old soul records and steal their spirit.

> —Bono, on the rock band U2's mission

Acting ain't brain surgery. But isn't it kinda neat that I can provide brain surgeons with some entertainment.

> —Actor Ken Wahl

The Church is a living orgasm.

> —New York Citizens Housing and Planning Council Chairman Robert Seavey, in his introduction of Cardinal John O'Connor

My neck was killing me after having to bop back and forth all day long. I told Jerry, "Now I know why you're so mean, man. Your neck hurts all the time."

> —Dennis Quaid, after playing Jerry Lee Lewis

Straight men don't have the time to spend with you, because they have to get laid, they have to work, and if they're married, they have to keep their marriages together.

> —Bette Midler, on why her close friends are women and gay men

Here's a guy that made noises twenty years ago of being some kind of spokesperson for a generation. I saw him on TV the other night, mud wrestling.
　　　　　　　—John Cougar Mellencamp, on Geraldo
　　　　　　　Rivera

Wouldn't you be insecure if she were your aunt? I saw her last Christmas, and she told me that I have no muscle tone in my thighs.
　　　　　　　—Bridget Fonda, on Aunt Jane

We were looking for something exciting to do, so we went to Vegas. We won some money and ended up at the Graceland Chapel, for Elvis, and that's what happened.
　　　　　　　—Jon Bon Jovi, on why he got married

I could say "loving my wife" or "the moment we exchanged wedding vows." But truthfully, acting's the best.
　　　　　　　—Corbin Bernsen of "L.A. Law,"
　　　　　　　explaining there's nothing better than
　　　　　　　acting

I guess they like short blond women with big boobs.
　　　　　　　—Dolly Parton, on why she's popular in
　　　　　　　Japan

The only happy artist is a dead artist, because only then you can't change. After I die, I'll probably come back as a paintbrush.
　　　　　　　—Sylvester Stallone

Frosted Shredded Wheat, Bartles & Jaymes, and any male whore cologne.
　　　　　　　—Sam Kinison, when asked which three
　　　　　　　products he'd like his picture on

The very meaning of a line in the law is that you intentionally may go as close to it as you can if you do not pass it.
> —The attorney for former House
> Speaker Jim Wright

How I love the society, the North American community, and the North American children.
> —General Manuel Noriega, Panamanian
> dictator, writing to an 11-year-old in
> Michigan

Every day it seems the devil walks through my door and I've got to run the son of a bitch out.
> —Dennis Quaid, on women trying to
> pick him up

If her household runs as perfectly as her press would have us believe, I'll slash my throat.
> —Susan Sarandon, on Meryl Streep

Outside of the killings, we have one of the lowest crime rates in the country.
> —Washington, D.C., Mayor Marion
> Barry

Hanging someone wasn't really something in our knowledge base.
> —An official of the Washington State
> Corrections Department, on the
> difficulty of finding a hangman for the
> first execution in twenty-six years

Strong women leave big hickeys.
> —Madonna

I could see it if you showed where I lived. But my parents aren't even on TV or in the movies. They don't ask for this.
> —Judd Nelson, whose parents' home has been egged, toilet papered, and spray painted by his fans

If you want to be really hip, you get married or check into a drug rehab center, or both.
> —Actor Eric Stoltz

I thought it was a significant development for American society.
> —Jim Wright, on why he inserted a plug for a motivational video in the *Congressional Record*—a video produced by a firm that employed his wife

This is how he found Dan Quayle, wasn't it?
> —Comedian Gary Shandling, after he was pulled from a line of White House tourists to meet the President

What do you want me to say . . . I'm going to make [the Alaskan oil spill] disappear?
> —Exxon chairman Lawrence Rawl, at annual meeting

TWENTY TONS OF DEAD SEA ANIMALS AND STILL COUNTING
> —Sign seen outside the Exxon meeting

Do you mind if I sit back a little? Because your breath is very
bad.

> —Donald Trump to Larry King, while
> appearing on King's radio show

Living.

> —Peter O'Toole, on what he hopes to be
> doing in ten years

Most of it is shit. Most of it is an audition to get on "Who's
the Boss."

> —Tim Robbins, on the theater scene in
> Los Angeles

I just love it that everyone is so rude here. It gives you the
complete freedom to be rude back. If you don't like someone, you can just scream at them.

> —British actress Joanne Whalley-
> Kilmer, on New Yorkers

Martin came in. He was not radically trying to change things,
but that's about where the parallel ends, because I don't
know what he did in his first hundred days.

> —George Bush, explaining why he said
> the first hundred days of his
> administration were "about the same
> as Martin Van Buren's"

IN THE CLEAR-THINKING DEPARTMENT

The time is right for some kind of action, but now we've got
to assess where we're going to go, what next step we take. We
take whatever the next step is.

> —George Bush, on the Middle East

We went to the meeting with low expectations. Like most Americans, we could have drawn up a long list of names of people qualified to be Vice President, and J. Danforth Quayle wouldn't have been on it. Well, we talked with him Monday. His name still wouldn't have been on it.

> —Editorial in the *Charlotte* (North Carolina) *Observer*

There's grounds for a defamation suit here. Not by Ollie. By Joe Isuzu.

> —A *New York Daily News* editorial, after prosecutor John Keker called Ollie North "the Joe Isuzu of government"

SLOGAN OF THE YEAR

Plead or bleed.

> —Texas Attorney General Jim Mattox, warning men who have fathered illegitimate children to acknowledge their paternity or be forced to take a blood test

What are you trying to do—get me killed?

> —Yasir Arafat, protesting an article about to run in an Arab newspaper that erroneously quoted him saying that the PLO charter was "null and void"

We can sell the '30s Reagan, but only because he was so young and some of the shots have him stripped to the waist and in Army boots.

> —A poster distributor, on the small
> demand for the ex-President's movie
> posters

THE FEUD

She had a tit job for sure. This is desperation. Well, maybe she'll get a job out of it.

> —Madonna, on La Toya Jackson's
> appearance in *Playboy*

Madonna is a no-talent. She slept with everybody on the way up. That's how she made it to the top.

> —La Toya Jackson, replying

In "Like a Prayer," she's the one who should have been crucified.

> —Jackson's manager, Jack Gordon,
> adding his two cents

There are a lot of things on CBS that I don't put there. You're on CBS, for chrissake.

> —"60 Minutes" producer Don Hewitt to
> Geraldo Rivera, during a forum on
> talk-show journalism

THE POT CALLING THE KETTLE BLACK

I find it extremely distasteful to listen to all this shouting.

> —Morton Downey, Jr., at the same
> forum

Listen to your majority and shut up.
> —Cybill Shepherd, an abortion-rights
> supporter, on what she'd like to say to
> George Bush

Throw to second, not first. Second is the one in the middle.
> —The coach of the Soviet National
> Baseball team, during a 21–1 loss to
> the U.S. Naval Academy

There was some rocking motion in the original. Perhaps two of our actors went overboard.
> —The producer of the film *Scandal,* on
> why an orgy scene had to be edited to
> avoid an X rating

We used to call it Mother's Day.
> —A crack dealer, on the lines that form
> at crack houses on the day welfare
> checks arrive

They're always relieved that Congress is not in session.
> —Arkansas Senator David Pryor, on the
> mood of his constituents during the
> Senate's summer recess

Twenty years from now, still another President will step before the lights of the TV cameras and tell us he has still another Great Drug Plan. By then the zombies will own the streets and we'll be shipping the dead to the rings of Neptune.
> —Columnist Pete Hamill

They made him bend over in front of all those men.
>—Tammy Faye Bakker, claiming her
>husband Jim was strip-searched

I heard he didn't respect the crown.
>—The "Miss America" pageant director,
>on why he didn't let last year's Miss
>America appear on "Late Night with
>David Letterman"

If you leave our gigs without your sexual glands being stirred, then you need therapy.
>—Bobby Dall, bass player for the rock
>group Poison

I came over on the Concorde for the first time, and I got slightly horny being in this plane with all these incredibly powerful men who deal in jillions of dollars.
>—Actress Theresa Russell

If I lose, I'm going to become a dancer at Chippendales [a Manhattan men's nude club for women].
>—New York Mayor Ed Koch, who did
>lose and may now be shopping for a
>G-string

It felt wonderful doing it. But that's rather like urinating in brown velvet pants. It can feel wonderful, but no one will watch.
>—Robin Williams, on appearing in *Dead
>Poets Society*

Given the things I said about Reagan—that he's a criminal who used the Constitution for toilet paper—it wouldn't surprise me if my phone was tapped.
—Actor John Cusack

Usually they send pictures; some of them are tempting. But I get some ugly ones, too. I give those to the home boys.
—Rap musician Ton-Loc

He was like a kid. Ask him to turn off a light, and by the time he gets to the switch, he's forgotten what he went for.
—Former campaign aide Joe Canzeri, on Dan Quayle

I'm not anti-American. I wave the flag as much as anyone else.
—An Army warrant officer convicted of spying for the Russians

YET ANOTHER SICK STORY

Two men in Long Island, New York, were arrested for robbing and fatally stabbing a nurse. As the cops inspected the loot, one of the suspects asked, "Do we get to keep the money that doesn't have blood on it?"

It's like a baby's bottom to which someone has affixed a pair of wire rims and a caterpillar.
—Film critic David Edelstein, describing "Weird Al" Yankovic

CIVIL RIGHTS, CHINA STYLE

It is necessary to form a deterrent force against them and develop a situation whereby, when a rat runs across the street, everybody cries, "Kill it!"
—A Chinese provincial governor, on prodemocracy demonstrators

YELLOW JOURNALISM, AMERICAN STYLE

Do you have visible wounds?
> —Former "Today" host Jane Pauley, to
> an escapee from the violence in China

HE'S GOT A POINT

In the 1960s and 1970s, there were many student movements and turmoils in the United States. Did they have any other recourse but to mobilize police and troops, arrest people, and shed blood?
> —Former Chinese Premier Deng
> Xiaoping

For some individuals, obtaining the scarce HUD subsidy funds was as easy as phoning Domino's for a pizza.
> —California Congressman Tom Lantos

Welcome to the world of being a sleaze.
> —Former securities trader accused of
> securities violations, to a business
> partner in a conversation secretly
> recorded by the FBI

THE REAGAN PRESIDENCY, IN A NUTSHELL

You go to bed every night knowing that there are things that you are not aware of.
> —Ronald Reagan

I always look forward to the opportunity to chop off more heads so that I can earn more money.
> —Saeed Al Sayyaf, Saudi Arabia's state executioner

Except for the noise the missiles and rockets create . . . we have no other problem.
> —A U.N. health worker, on playing golf at the Kabul (Afghanistan) Golf and Country Club

Assault weapons for the middle class.
> —California gun dealer Richard Bash, on the specialty of his shop

Think springtime, Bryant. Four more days and the little croci will begin to poke their heads up your shorts.
> —Willard Scott to Bryant Gumbel on "Today"

No, he has a meeting with Henry Kissinger.
> —White House spokesperson Marvin Fitzwater, when asked if President Bush had "anything significant" on his schedule

The most famous welfare mother in the world.
> —Pete Hamill, on Princess Di

There was a time in my life when I spent 90 percent of my money on booze and broads. And the rest of it I just wasted.
> —Freshman Georgia Representative Ben Jones, former star of the TV show "The Dukes of Hazzard"

I made the movie, they gave me my money, thank you. I never saw it. I never heard of it—and you know, as far as I'm concerned, it never existed. Thanks! Good-bye!

> —Christopher Walken, on his film *War Zone*

IN THE MODESTY DEPARTMENT

"Miami Vice" has opened up the world for me and given me a sense of immortality.

> —Philip Michael Thomas

I never used to like babies. I mean, I'd always think, "Well, if a baby were more like a chimpanzee, I'd have one."

> —Candice Bergen, who in fact did go on to have a baby

When I got through with the twin pregnancy my abdominal skin was such that I had to fold it up and then stick it in my pants.

> —Cybill Shepherd

I think I was born an alcoholic. The story is that I got drunk at my christening.

> —John Larroquette, who's been on the wagon for seven years

Between the panty hose and the corset, if you want to take a piss, that's a twenty-minute thing.

> —Harvey Fierstein, on his transsexual wardrobe in *Torch Song Trilogy*

I can name a few stars I have worked with who have actually fooled people into thinking they're incredibly talented.
—Dennis Quaid

Actors shouldn't marry each other. The only people who should do that are people who work with hazardous nuclear materials.
—Bill Murray

I'm less sexually jealous than average. On the other hand, lust is very high on the list, very high indeed.
—John Cleese, star of *A Fish Named Wanda*

I felt so sorry for him. I thought, "This poor man is going through all of this for just half a nipple."
—La Toya Jackson, on the photographer who took her pictures for *Playboy*

This is a ladies' man? He looks like Yoda with a bad haircut.
—Jay Leno, on former Texas Senator John Tower

My whole problem is I'm not afraid to make commitments.
—Rock star Steve Earle, on why he's been married five times

The most beautiful woman in the world can look like dogshit on camera. Fortunately for me, it also works the other way around.
—Mel Gibson, on why he's a sex symbol

If all you have in life is bad choices, crack may not be the most unpleasant of them.
> —*New Republic* writer Jefferson Morley, after trying crack

I am afraid of lesbians.
> —Zsa Zsa Gabor, on why she didn't want to go to jail

INSTANT INDIGESTION

It reconstitutes very well.
> —TWA executive Art Dupree, on why the airline prefers thigh meat to white meat in chicken dishes

As a teenager, I crept around on eggshells because people kept telling me I could destroy men.
> —Cybill Shepherd

Women feel dirty; men don't.
> —Jerry Hall, on sex without love

NO, WE WON'T ASK ABOUT 1990

Life will be like a happening episode of "The Jetsons."
> —Debbie Gibson, when asked about what she expected 1989 would bring

We need to look at all the places dirty deposits can cause trouble.
> —Exxon ad

I've never been in a room with so many people who should be in jail.

> —Show-business agent Sam Cohn, on the Cannes Film Festival

There's no moral problem there. I used to teach ethics—trust me.

> —Drug czar William Bennett, on the idea that drug dealers should be decapitated

Don't drop them.

> —Queen Elizabeth, handing the symbols of his new knighthood to Ronald Reagan

If that plane doesn't fly, the debate is over. It is far too expensive to be a Stealth taxi.

> —Senator Sam Nunn, on defense spending logic

2

NOW, THAT'S A CRIME

IN THE MOTHER-OF-THE-YEAR DEPARTMENT . . .

A 21-year-old Phoenix woman was sentenced to eight months in jail for leaving her 18-month-old daughter locked in a closet for eight days when she went to the hospital to have another baby. Fortunately, the toddler survived.

SELF-KNOWLEDGE IS A WONDERFUL THING

A 22-year-old man allegedly broke into a home in Hammond, Indiana, to burglarize the place. He gathered up a few items, then decided he needed a little nap. The homeowners returned, found him sound asleep in a chair, then called the police. When the cops woke the man and asked him what he was doing there, he replied, "What can I say? I'm a poor burglar."

BIGGEST BUST OF THE YEAR

Acting on a tip, Greenwich, Connecticut, police stopped a car carrying a 34-year-old man. When he exited the car, the cops noticed something very unmanly about his figure. When they strip-searched him, they discovered the strapping man was wearing a bra and panties—stuffed with more than 125 vials of crack. Let us guess—the bra was a C cup?

THE MOST-INEPT-BANK-ROBBER-OF-THE-YEAR AWARD . . .

. . . goes to a Brooklyn, New York, man. According to New York City police, the man's demeanor was so meek that he was able to persuade tellers to turn over money in only seven of twenty-five bank robbery attempts. On one typical day, he handed threatening letters to tellers at four banks, but walked away with a grand total of $363 from one bank. Mr. "Meek's" saga came to an end on a rare occasion when he left with cash, which turned out to be a packet of bills wrapped around a device that explodes and leaves a residue that identifies the suspect. It did and he was.

THE POLICE ACADEMY AWARD FOR OUTSTANDING LAW ENFORCEMENT . . .

. . . goes to two cops in Hayward, California, who mistook the cane of a blind man for an illegal martial arts weapon. David St. John, unable to see the uniforms of the police, thought he was being mugged when he heard two men demand that he empty his pockets. He resisted, and the cops beat him with their nightsticks.

DISCOUNT FOR JESUS TOO DEVILISH

Gas station owner Jerry Harrison of Pensacola, Florida, faced six months in jail. The charge: violating visual clutter laws by erecting a sign advertising a 10 percent discount to "those who love Jesus." Anybody think the cops in Pensacola have too much time on their hands?

DISCRETION IS ADVISED

No doubt more than a few people have turned to the privacy of a hotel room for various kinds of hankie-pankie, as a Queens, New York, couple allegedly did when they checked into a Quality Inn in Bristol, Connecticut. Shortly before midnight, however, guests at the hotel spotted the couple running naked through the parking lot, and they began to dial the management. A few minutes later, police found the romping couple back in their hotel room—along with both crack and cocaine.

WHEN IT PAYS TO GRIN AND BEAR IT

A Selma, Alabama, man laid out some hard-earned cash for crack. When he opened the vial, he discovered he'd purchased soap. The man was so outraged that he marched to the nearest police station to file a fraud complaint against the drug dealer. Instead, police tossed him in the slammer while they checked to see what charges they could file against him.

THIRSTIEST BANDIT OF THE YEAR . . .

. . . had to have been a man who walked into a Tulsa, Oklahoma, convenience store, whipped out a gun, pointed it at the clerk—and demanded a single beer. The cops arrived in time to collar the thief, who had just finished consuming the evidence.

ANOTHER MOTHER-OF-THE-YEAR AWARD CANDIDATE . . .

. . . is a New York City woman who decided to help her 3-month-old daughter go to sleep by lacing her milk with methadone. The baby nearly died and the mother ended up in the slammer.

DEPUTY DEBACLE

Here's the scoop from Pinon Hills, California. A sheriff's deputy was estranged from his wife, a sheriff's deputy, when he found out she was having an affair—with a sheriff's deputy. So the deputy shot the deputy and the deputy, then committed deputy-cide.

ANOTHER BURGLAR-OF-THE-YEAR CONTESTANT

A 22-year-old man was weaving his way down the streets of North Bellmore, New York, when he allegedly decided to burgle to buy another bottle. He crawled through a front window and searched the rooms. Then the exertion and the ninety-degree heat evidently got to him. The lady of the house came home a little later to find this stalwart criminal sleeping naked on the couch.

THE BATTERED-LESBIAN DEFENSE

In a number of widely publicized trials, women who have suffered severe physical abuse from spouses have won acquittal on murder charges by arguing that their husbands would have killed them if they hadn't acted in self-defense. In 1989, that defense was put forward by the abused partner in a lesbian relationship in Palm Beach County, Florida. According to attorneys for the defendant, Annette Green shot and killed her lover, Ivonne Julio, who had assumed the masculine role in the homosexual relationship, because she believed Julio would kill her.

THE NAGGING-WIFE DEFENSE

Harry Garfinkle, 78, was arrested for strangling his bedridden 84-year-old wife, Frances. However, Garfinkle told the authorities that his wife had nagged at him unmercifully for the more than ten years she'd been ill. So he was allowed to plead guilty to involuntary manslaughter and was placed on probation. The judge told him, "Try to go along enjoying your life."

Anyone out there whose fingers are tingling a bit?

SAVED BY THE BELL

It must have been a very nervous or very inexperienced armed robber who walked into Mrs. Winner's Chicken and Biscuits restaurant in Birmingham, Alabama. The desperado had herded the employees together and was demanding money from the cashier when the bell on the biscuit timer jingled. The robber, mistaking the bell for a burglar alarm, panicked and fled. According to the Associated Press, "the biscuits came out golden brown."

GRANDPARENTS OF THE YEAR

The grandparents of a 4-year-old boy in Muskogee, Oklahoma, were arrested for confining the boy to a fenced-in pen all day, every day. The pen had no roof and contained no toilet facilities.

HE'S IN LOVE WITH MATRI-MONEY

California cops finally nailed America's most notorious Don Juan—pudgy 45-year-old Louis Carlucci. Carlucci, whose exploits had been profiled on NBC's "Unsolved Mysteries," had allegedly secured more than $1 million from an estimated thirty-five wives he'd married and abandoned. Along the way, Carlucci also had fathered an estimated thirty-five children. That's energy.

"BANKMAN'S" CAUGHT ROBBIN'

An Orlando, Florida, bank robber, evidently inspired by Jack Nicholson's dazzling performance as the Joker in *Batman*, donned heavy white makeup and eyeliner, bright red lipstick, and a yellow rhinestone T-shirt and began sticking up local banks. The alleged copycat was so proud of himself that he engaged in what cops called "verbal diarrhea," leading to his arrest.

ZEBU-CIDE

Authorities in Buffalo, New York, offered a $5,500 reward for information leading to the arrest of a party or parties who broke into the children's zoo and beat to death a zebu, a gentle oxlike animal.

THE SHOW MUST GO ON . . .

Gordon Benjamin, an inmate in a Massachusetts state prison, turned down the offer of parole so he could play Lancelot in an inmate production of *Camelot*.

CARRY ME BACK TO OLE VIRGINIE

Vice cops in Washington, D.C., frustrated at turnstile justice that returned prostitutes to the streets hours after their convictions, rounded up a large group of hookers in one section of the Capitol and marched them 1.4 miles over the line into Virginia. Virginia authorities were not amused, and neither were police brass.

And the streetwalkers? They were back in place in half an hour.

WHY AREN'T WE SURPRISED?

Federal and New York City investigators found hundreds of human body parts amid four tons of medical waste at a

Brooklyn, New York, carting company that has been linked to organized crime.

ANOTHER MOTHER-OF-THE-YEAR CANDIDATE . . .

A 17-year-old girl was arrested in Liberty, New York, for abandoning her newborn baby deep in the woods shortly after his birth. The story had a miraculous ending, however—somehow the tot managed to live for five days until he was found.

HEATED WORDS

A woman and two teenagers tried to collect a drug debt by forcing a flaming blowtorch down the throat of a Providence, Rhode Island, woman—while her 8-year-old son watched.

IN THE NAME OF THE LORD, WE EMBEZZLETH THESE FUNDS

A live-in maid in Bartow, Florida, was arrested on charges of stealing $800,000 from the paraplegic widow she worked for. Most of the money was given to a TV ministry.

YET ANOTHER MOTHER-OF-THE-YEAR CANDIDATE

A Stamford, Connecticut, woman was sentenced to ten years in jail for allowing a drug dealer to rape her 10-year-old daughter in exchange for crack.

MAYBE IT WAS WISHFUL THINKING

A New York City man was arrested as he stopped at the office of his insurance company to pick up a $170,793 payment of a life insurance policy on his wife. The problem: she wasn't dead.

VIOLATION

A Brooklyn, New York, taxi driver was arrested on charges of criminal mischief stemming from his hobby—which happened to be pouring acid into the change slots of parking meters. Before the man was arrested, he destroyed more than two hundred meters' worth over $300,000.

DRIP-DRIES

A man wanted in connection with shooting a New York policeman was arrested after he was found hiding in a clothes dryer in a Florida house. The police had to disassemble the appliance to remove the man.

FOR A MADAGASCAR HISSING ROACH, YOU CAN GET A NEW YORK LAWYER

How much does it cost to hire an attorney in Indiana? About eighteen snakes—or at least it did in the case of a man who faced drug charges. When the defendant told the court he couldn't pay for a lawyer, the judge ordered him to dispose of his reptile collection, which included rattlesnakes and boa constrictors—which he kept in his apartment.

21 JUMP STREET UPDATE

In what must have been an embarrassing moment, a 25-year-old undercover police officer posing as a high school student was spanked by the school's principal for being late for classes. If we were that principal, we'd be *very* careful not to speed on the way home.

NEW MATH

A Los Angeles high school English teacher allegedly decided he'd help solve the mathematical illiteracy of today's youth. His method—booking sports bets for his students. Authorities weren't amused.

McBUNGLE

A customer who pulled up to the drive-in window of a McDonalds in Euclid, Ohio, must have been surprised to find that instead of a burger and fries, the bag contained all of the day's receipts of the restaurant. No one knows for sure, because the customer never returned to complain. And since the loss was a mix-up rather than a robbery, police told McDonalds that the customer couldn't be charged with a crime.

McDONALDS GUNMAN SHOT IN THE BUNS

No, the story's not as good as the headline. A teenage armed robber stole the night receipts at a fast-food outlet in Brooklyn, New York. On his way out of the store, he ran into an ex-cop, who shot the robber twice in the backside.

YOU LIGHT UP MY LIFE

An Akron, Ohio, man doused his pregnant daughter with brake fluid, then set her aflame. Shortly afterward, the girl gave birth—to a healthy baby girl.

DID HE GET TO KEEP THE MILK CARTON?

Tom Lawson of Tulsa, Oklahoma, distributed thousands of flyers nationwide in an attempt to find his missing 16-year-old son. He was elated when he received a call telling him his son was in Fort Lauderdale, Florida. Lawson flew in and was met at the airport by a man who took him to a remote location, robbed him of his wallet, money, watch, and credit cards, and abandoned him.

YOU GOTTA WONDER WHAT HIS PROBLEM WAS

A thief broke into a K-Mart store in Janesville, Wisconsin, and got away with 432 jars of lip balm—nothing else.

THE SHERLOCK HOLMES AWARD FOR GREAT POLICE DETECTION

Police announced that they'd decided that the death of David Christian Agar was "suspicious." That was a few days after his body was found in the street wrapped in duct tape from head to toe.

THE CASE FOR ABORTION

A 13-year-old Garland, Texas, boy stole his parents' car one day and went for a joyride. He was eventually arrested by police. His parents arrived, arranged for his release, and got him in the car to drive home. The grateful lad then pulled a knife, forced his parents out of the car, and took off again.

MAYBE HE JUST WANTED AN AGENT

A convicted bank robber escaped from a U.S. penitentiary. Then, for some unexplained reason, he underwent a series of plastic surgery operations so he could look like actor Robert DeNiro. Unfortunately, the expense was in vain, as he was nabbed in Florida. Maybe he should have chosen another celebrity, say, Roberta Flack.

WORST TIPPER OF THE YEAR

They were described by neighbors as just two typical suburban kids—until they got into crack. Then the 18-year-old girl and the 20-year-old man began to make frequent trips from Scotch Plains, New Jersey, to New York's Lower East Side. The girl's father became so concerned he removed the distributor cap from her car one night so she couldn't drive. Undaunted, the pair took the train to the city. Late that night, they offered a cab driver $175 to drive them home. When the cab got to Scotch Plains, the girl allegedly pulled out a .38-calibre revolver and killed the cab driver.

YOU WANT TO KNOW HOW DANGEROUS NEW YORK REALLY IS?

A 49-year-old man allegedly walked into a Brooklyn bank, handed the teller a threatening note, and walked out with $2,100. But he only got a few steps before he was mugged, losing the entire $2,100. Even criminals aren't safe anymore!

FRIDAY THE 13TH, PART 735

A 31-year-old suburban Chicago physician began to believe that he was cursed because he'd been born on Friday the 13th. One night, he awoke, then began slashing his wife with an ax until she was dead. Then he drowned their 2½-month-old baby in the bathtub because he didn't want her growing up without a mother. Needless to say, a court ruled the doctor was insane.

SORRY, SANTA

A St. Paul, Minnesota, man made so much money selling drugs that he'd often drive down the street tossing cash to children out of the windows. Unfortunately for the dealer, one of his drives was videotaped by the cops. An investigation led to a fifteen-year sentence on drug charges, announced by a judge who said that the man's acts might convince children "that drug-dealing was a profitable activity to be emulated."

IF THEY ASK FOR A DANCE, DON'T REFUSE

What's human life worth? Very little, at least to some young people. Like the three teenage girls from Fort Worth, Texas, who wanted to go to a nightclub but lacked transportation. So they went into a convenience store, shot the clerk to death, and stole her car.

HOMEMAKER OF THE YEAR

The first thing cops do after collaring a suspect is read him his rights. However, when two New York City police officers burst into an apartment, they discovered the man they sought was a voodoo priest. The cops found human skulls hanging from a cross, jars of internal organs, chicken legs, and a potato sack full of bones. What did they do? Said one, "I asked the guy not to put a hex on me. He said he understood we were doing our jobs."

LASSIE GO HOME

What would you do if a park ranger stopped you for letting your dog run around without a leash? Well, a Manhattan woman defended her pet in typical canine fashion—she bit the ranger.

EASY AS TAKING CRACK FROM A BABY

Police moved in to bust a 28-year-old man for dealing drugs while standing outside his car. But when they searched the man, they didn't find any drugs. They were on the verge of setting him free when his girlfriend's 16-month-old son, who was sitting in a car seat, held up his little hand—which contained a couple vials of crack.

SORRY ABOUT THAT

Noel Pagan served three years in jail for stabbing Mark Weaver, causing injuries so severe that Weaver has since been in a coma. With no hope of recovery for him, Weaver's family has sought court permission to remove the man from life support. Hearing the news, Pagan filed legal papers to stop the action. The reason: If Weaver dies, Pagan could be rearrested for murder. The court had precious little sympathy.

FRED, THERE'S A NAKED LADY OUTSIDE OUR WINDOW

Teresa Wyatt, age 65, looked out her seventeenth-floor apartment window one night to see a naked, screaming lady hanging precariously from a cable TV wire. She hurriedly woke her husband, and the two grabbed the woman, holding on for ten long minutes until other neighbors could help pull her to safety. The woman told police that she'd been raped by a gang, then forced to jump off the twenty-one-story-high rooftop. Only the miraculous grab of the cable saved her life.

THE WILLIE HORTON AWARD

An Indiana man imprisoned for beating his ex-wife was given a weekend pass for "good behavior." He allegedly took the opportunity to locate his ex-wife and beat her to death with a shotgun. Despite the man's threats, prison authorities had not felt compelled to tell the woman that her ex-husband was being released for two days.

SEE SPOT SHOT

In a precedent-setting case, the owner of a pit bull that mauled a 2-year-old boy to death was charged with murder by a California court—the first time owners of the dangerous animal have been held responsible for vicious attacks.

L'EGGS DIAMOND

A robber wearing a pantyhose mask seized an employee of Arby's in West Valley City, Utah, believing that she carried a bag containing the night's receipts. But he didn't count on two things: first, that the girl's boyfriend, a high school football player, would be there to grab him, wrestle him inside, and strip off his mask; and two, that another employee would recognize him—as her husband.

HERE, BOY

The judge called it a "mean act." Other people could find stronger words for the Delaware River Port Authority police officer who was fired for tossing a stray dog off a bridge into the river.

YOUR HONOR, WE CALL MISTER ED

A Fairfield, Pennsylvania, man was arrested on charges of drunken driving and driving without lights when he and the Appaloosa he was riding were struck from behind by a pickup truck. The charges were dismissed, however, when the driver's lawyer told the court, "A horse is a horse, of course, of course." The judge agreed that horses are not mentioned in the motor vehicle laws.

ATTENTION K-MART SHOPPERS

K-Mart was ordered to pay $2.4 million to the shooting victim of a man who had walked into one of its branches, drunk, to purchase the murder weapon.

TONGUE-TWISTING CRIME CAPER

Federal Customs agents in New York seized 8,000 pounds of marijuana that had been packed in 100-pound cans of jalapeño peppers. Quipped a Customs agent, "You could say Customs picked pot packed in pickled peppers."

MURDER MOST FOWL

We couldn't resist the headline. The story: A North Olmsted, Ohio, man was sentenced by a judge to two months of community service for running over a beloved neighborhood duck with his car.

DUMBO

A 14-year-old boy and an 11-year-old boy were arrested in Temple Hills, Maryland, after a week-long rampage in which they played "Rambo" by dressing in camouflage clothing, then stalking the woods firing .22-calibre rifles at cars, street lights, and buildings. Fortunately, no one was seriously injured.

KIDDIE CAPER

Police in Westminster, Colorado, were called to haul in two burglars who were caught removing a grocery cart full of jewelry, cash, food, and other valuables from an apartment. The thieves, who had removed a screen to gain access to an unlocked window, were a 5-year-old girl and her 4-year-old brother.

MAYBE HE WANTED TO PLAY SANTA CLAUS

A man from Long Island was arrested for stealing $7,330 in "play money" from a Toys 'R' Us store. The money can be redeemed only for merchandise sold in the store.

PARTY ANIMAL

A 52-year-old Dunn, North Carolina, man set an unofficial world record when he was picked up on his thirty-third drunken-driving arrest. The astounded judge took one look at his twenty-one-page rap sheet and tossed him in the slammer for seven years.

3

BOY, IS THAT DUMB! THE 1989 DAN QUAYLE AWARDS

POLICE HUMOR

Homicide detectives in Saratoga Springs, New York, were spotted wearing buttons that read, "OUR DAY BEGINS WHEN YOURS ENDS."

OKAY, BUT HE DOES LOOK A LITTLE LIKE ROBERT REDFORD

Vice-President Dan Quayle raised more than a few eyebrows during a speech at the Young Republicans National Convention when he announced that America would soon celebrate the twentieth anniversary of "Neil Armstrong and Buzz Lukens's walk on the moon." You see, Buzz Lukens is the Ohio congressman sentenced to jail after his conviction for having sex with a 16-year-old girl. Quayle meant to refer to astronaut Buzz Aldrin—or did he?

POLICE PLANT

The problem: Thieves in Hilo, Hawaii, are making off with prize plants from public parks in record numbers.

The solution: Marking the plants with yellow paint to discourage thieves.

The question: Do tourists really want to tour gardens to see plants splattered with yellow paint?

THE EDUCATION OF DANNY QUAYLE

Dan Quayle's academic record is less than exemplary, so it's natural that the Administration would want the Vice-President to catch up on his American history. Quayle, however, reportedly chose an unusual method—riding horseback over the National Battlefield Park, where the famous Battles of Bull Run were fought. While this pastime seems harmless, critics charge that scarce government funds were being spent to maintain a stable of ten horses solely for the use of Quayle, his family, and Secret Service agents at a time when three park staff members had been laid off and some tours and other activities had been canceled. The park supervisor explained that the general public is prohibited from riding the horses, but Quayle and his family are a "different situation." A former park historian calls the history lessons a "boondoggle." Some people have gone so far as to suggest the government could save money if Quayle simply read a book on the Civil War—then again, the VP doesn't seem to do too well with books.

YOU CAN'T JUDGE A BOOK BY ITS COVER

John Barrier was dressed in his dirty construction clothes when he walked into the Old National Bank in Spokane, Washington, to get a parking ticket validated. A teller looked at him like he crawled out from under a rock and refused, telling him that he'd have to make a deposit. Barrier protested that he was a substantial customer of the bank, but both the teller and a manager refused to stamp the ticket. Understandably angry, Barrier withdrew his funds—a whopping $2 million. Wonder what bank brass had to say to the manager who refused to stamp the ticket?

GREAT MOMENTS IN AMERICAN CRIME

Three men in Greensboro, North Carolina, were evidently so busy planning and executing the burglary of a convenience store that they failed to notice one small detail—their crime was carried out right after a fresh snowfall. When the robbery was reported the next day, police followed their tracks a quarter-mile to their apartment door. Adding insult to arrest was the fact that the brilliant career criminals found the store's cash register completely empty.

DRUMMING UP BUSINESS

An Annapolis, Maryland, fireman was very bored one day when two teenagers called the fire station. So he jokingly told the pair to set a fire. The two boys promptly torched a vacant house, and the fireman was forced to ante up $1,630 to pay the damages.

GREAT MOMENTS IN EDUCATION

After protests, school officials yanked a creative coloring workbook that asked special education students to pretend they were criminals by drawing a mug shot of themselves.

OH, BUILD US A HOME, WHERE THE DODO BIRDS ROAM . . .

A single San Diego horned lizard, member of an endangered species, was spotted on the site of a planned industrial park four years ago. No sightings have been reported since. But that didn't stop the California Fish and Game Department from ordering the site's developers to pay for creation of a new habitat for the lizard—in case it ever shows up.

AN EENSY-WEENSY LITTLE COMPUTER ERROR

A Muskogee, Oklahoma, man was selected at random by a computer for jury duty at a murder trial. One tiny problem— he was the defendant.

IS TANG REALLY WORTH THAT MUCH?

The family of a Navy Lieutenant Commander was awarded $300,000 by a court for a claim that the officer's daughter's improper expulsion from a school created such turmoil that he failed a test, ruining his chance to become an astronaut. Huh?

BLEEDING HEART GORED AGAIN

The Reverend Marshall Gourley of Denver tried to stem the tide of violence by offering $100 to anyone who turned over a firearm to him. That offer aroused the capitalist instincts of Robin Heid. Heid bought a handgun for $40, turned it over to Gourley, collected his C note, then used it as a down payment on an assault rifle.

SCOTCH, NO ICE

A New York gem dealer allegedly failed to exercise good judgment while waiting in Los Angeles International Airport for a plane back home. He walked into a bar, ordered four drinks, then began to feel lightheaded. He made it to the rest room, where he passed out. When he woke up, something was missing—his briefcase, which contained a cool $1.2 million in diamonds.

THE JEAN VALJEAN AWARD

Like the Canadian Mounted Police, the Morris County, New Jersey, DA's office always gets their man. That's why an investigator spent fourteen years tracking down Roy Andrew Rafos, who skipped town after his conviction. The investigator traced the fugitive to Springville, Alabama, where he had a wife, family, and a reputable business.

What was the crime that triggered this manhunt? Ramos was convicted for urinating on a convenience store wall. Evidently, New Jersey has no unsolved murders, rapes, burglaries, frauds, thefts, or other felonies to worry about.

STILL ANOTHER MOTHER-OF-THE-YEAR CANDIDATE

... is the Staten Island, New York, mother who allowed her 2-year-old child to play out in the backyard, unattended, with her pet wolf. The wolf attacked the child, causing wounds that will require years of plastic surgery to heal.

IF YOU BELIEVE THIS, YOU'LL BELIEVE ANYTHING

The daughter of Defense Secretary Richard Cheney was declared ineligible for a summer job at Yellowstone National Park—until her mother got her hired by calling the superintendent of the park. The Cheneys insisted, however, that their political connections had nothing to do with the change in decision. Said Mrs. Cheney, "I wasn't calling as somebody in Washington. I was calling as a mother."

QUAYLE AND THE CADETS

The Vice-President, who's military record involves defending cornfields in Indiana during the Vietnam War, was allegedly hissed by cadets when he gave a speech at West Point's commencement. Afterward, the VP's staff stepped in to attempt to forestall publicity. Said David Beckwith, Quayle's press secretary, "They made an animal-type grunting sound when the National Guard was mentioned. There were some good-natured grunts. Let me admit theoretically that some people hissed."

A VERY DIFFERENT PRISON BREAK

Many movies have featured hardened cons breaking out of the big house. So maybe the one consolation shared by three would-be burglars may be selling movie rights to their unusual story. According to police, the three allegedly attempted to steal a pickup truck in Larkspur, California. The truck owner unexpectedly returned and caught them in the act. He hailed a police car, which gave chase. In their frantic efforts to escape, the three men evidently didn't realize that the tall fence they scaled was the outer fence of someplace they didn't want to be. Inadvertently, they had broken into San Quentin Prison. Prison guards soon nabbed them.

YOUR TAX DOLLARS AT WORK

Every state indulges in the same silliness, but the New York State legislature seems to spend more time considering bills naming "official state" whatevers. For example, New York has an official state muffin, an official state beverage, an official state fruit, and an official state fossil. Among the bills entered this year were ones naming an official state bug (the ladybug), an official state patriot (a meat packer named Samuel Wilson), and an official state bottle (an Empire Spring mineral water vessel made shortly before 1900). We vote that any legislator who introduces these bills should be labeled "Official State Nuisance."

NEXT, THEY'LL GO AFTER VOODOO PRIESTS

The Atlantic City, New Jersey, city council passed a law requiring all palm readers to undergo a licensing procedure that includes a criminal background check. Nothing worse than having a bunch of felonious palm readers running around.

YOUR TAX DOLLARS STILL AT WORK

Among the most inexplicable policies of the American government are regulations that require communities to house homeless families in motels rather than rent them apartments or homes. One example: Westchester County, New York, the county immediately north of New York City, has more homeless families than available motel spaces. So they're shipping families to Orange County. The tab: $52,195 per year for two rooms for a family, plus a daily $220 round-trip cab fare to take the family's children back to Westchester County to go to school.

IN THE STUPID CORPORATE PRIDE DEPARTMENT . . .

Honors are shared by fifteen major airlines who had the audacity to cut a crucial scene in the Oscar-award-winning movie *Rain Man*. The reason for butchering a work of art: Dustin Hoffman, playing an autistic savant, refuses to board an airplane because he's memorized statistics about airplane crashes. Next thing we know, we'll find newspapers with whole articles removed at airport newsstands.

IN THE WISHFUL THINKING DEPARTMENT . . .

In Oklahoma City, Oklahoma, a truck driver sold 299 color television sets from the back of his truck for $50 to $60 apiece. The FBI broadcast an appeal that purchasers return the hot

TVs in exchange for a promise that they wouldn't be prosecuted. Nobody responded. Now, isn't that amazing?

IN THE STUPID LEGISLATION DEPARTMENT . . .

State Senator Tim Mathern is concerned that the name *North Dakota* conveys an image of blizzards and other severe climactic conditions. So he introduced resolutions that would change the name of the state to *Dakota*, which means *friend* in the Sioux language. Mathern failed to explain how the name change would help the weather.

DO THEY REALLY DRIVE ON THE WRONG SIDE OF THE ROAD IN LONDON?

City fathers in London, Ohio, were red-faced after it was revealed that the city accidentally sold a municipal parking garage for $51,555. The city authorized the sale of an adjoining property without realizing the deed included the garage. Now they have to buy it back or lease it.

BUT WOULD SHE WANT TO?

Residents of Seattle were not amused when the State Film and Video Office placed an ad in movie trade publications urging filmmakers to shoot in Seattle. Their objection: The ad's headline read DEBBIE COULD HAVE DONE DALLAS IN SEATTLE, a reference to a very famous pornographic movie.

DUM, DE DUM DUM

A rather dimwitted thief broke into a San Francisco museum to steal three priceless Soviet artifacts—a silver gift cross, a gospet setting, and gold jewelry. What he got were holograms, three-dimensional laser pictures of the objects that were etched on a plate of glass. Officials compared the theft to dating a picture from *Playboy* rather than the real model herself.

BUT DO WE GET TO KEEP "JINGLE BELLS"?

The official hymnal of the new Presbyterian Church will not contain "Onward Christian Soldiers" and "Battle Hymn of the Republic" because they were deemed "too military." "God Rest Ye Merry Gentlemen" was booted because it allegedly contained sexist overtones. Rumor has it "We Three Kings" will be next to go, because it's not clear that the Wise Men paid sales tax on their gifts.

AMERICA'S AMBASSADORS TO THE WORLD

The new Bush Administration came under a lot of fire when more than 75 percent of the new foreign ambassadors named turned out to be political appointees rather than foreign service professionals. Among the shining examples were:

- Peter Secchia, Ambassador to Italy. Among the remarks attributed to Secchia:

  I saw the new Italian Navy. Its boats have glass bottoms, so they can see the old Italian Navy.

  I need a big-titted woman to dance this one with (when the band at a party struck up a tune).

  I'm so proud of my fucking candidates I could shit (at a Michigan Republican gathering).

Secchia's mouth won him the label in the Italian press of "the ambassador of dirty words."

- Chic Hecht, Ambassador to the Bahamas. This former one-term Congressman had been known primarily for his verbal gaffes, such as his pledge that there would be no "nuclear suppository" in his state. In response to a Senate committee inquiry as to his qualifications, Hecht replied, "Lifestyle for the Commonwealth of the Bahamas is similar to the lifestyle of Las Vegas, Nevada."

- Della Newman, Ambassador to New Zealand. Newman, a Seattle real estate broker, told a New Zealand paper that she had no particular interest in foreign affairs and couldn't name that country's prime minister.

COP SILENCES DRUG DEALERS, LOSES JOB

A New Jersey police chief was so fed up with seeing drug dealers do business out of three public telephone booths that he cut the lines going into the phones. Evidently, the telephone company sorely missed the business, because they filed charges against the chief. The anti-drug warrior was convicted, which means that he's banned from police work for life. Good job, New Jersey Bell.

GOD IS MY CO-DEFENDANT

Many aspects of our everyday lives have been clouded by the threat of somebody filing a lawsuit. The most ridiculous consequence we've heard is a decision by Burlington County, New Jersey, not to plant any more trees because officials are afraid that motorists will run into the trees and sue the county. In that case, why don't they go one better and just close all the roads?

C.O.D. (CLODS ON DUTY)

A 47-year-old mailman was suspended for two weeks by the Postal Service for using the term *junk mail*. The service insists on the term *bulk-rate business mail*. We call their decision *bulk-rate bull waste*.

IN THE VERY DUMB BANK ROBBER DEPARTMENT

A man who robbed the Key Bank in Syracuse, New York, was arrested shortly afterward. The reason: He left an envelope containing his wife's car loan papers at the teller's window.

BUBBA BROUHAHA

The Arkansas General Assembly, for the first time in recorded history, found itself without a single representative nicknamed Bubba. Immediately, two representatives introduced legislation that said, "a session of the Arkansas General Assembly without a Bubba is like Christmas without a Claus . . . like a health clinic without condoms . . . and like Jim without Tammy." The resolution went on to name an *Arkansas Gazette* columnist named Bubba an honorary representative. Aren't you Arkansas folks happy your elected officials have such important tasks to accomplish? Now, where are they giving out condoms?

MARKSMAN-OF-THE-YEAR HONORS . . .

. . . goes to a Brightwater, New York, man who walked into a video store crowded with fifty people, opened fire with a Chinese assault rifle—and didn't hit a soul.

DEMOCRACY AT WORK

There evidently was a shortage of civic interest in the Joint Creek Water Improvement District election in Arlie, Oregon. The vote tally was 0—that's right, nobody voted. Nonvoters included all five of the candidates for seats on the District Board.

IN THE OUTRAGEOUS LEGAL DECISIONS DEPARTMENT

A Long Island woman abandoned her husband and 2-year-old son thirteen years ago. The husband raised the boy without one single contact—no letters, no phone calls—from the mother. Then at age 15, the boy was killed in a tragic bicycle accident. The mother showed up, claiming half of a $300,000 payment on a life insurance policy. The court, of course, gave it to her.

THE DUMBEST FUGITIVE OF THE YEAR

A Brooklyn, New York, man was shrewd enough to allegedly embezzle more than one million dollars during his employment as a New York City auditor. When he found himself facing arrest, he fled. To elude authorities, the auditor put on a great deal of weight, grew a beard, and repeatedly changed his wardrobe. However, he made one slight mistake—the cops caught up with him in a Florida hotel where he had registered under his own name.

THE DUMBEST CONVICTS

Ten Columbus, Ohio, inmates were being driven from one jail to another when they discovered an amazing trick—the clip on the prison van's seat belts could be used to break their handcuffs. Now, that was smart. What was dumb was that when the van arrived at the destination, the ten held up their hands proudly to a sheriff's deputy and said, "See what we did." Not only did they lose a chance to escape and alert all jail authorities to the threat, but they also faced charges of destroying government property.

DAN DOESN'T QUIVER

I stand by all the misstatements.
> —Dan Quayle, on gaffes uncounted and uncountable

A VICTORY FOR THE ANT AND ROACH LOBBY

Bowing to pressure, the Black Flag company said it would no longer play taps over dead ants and roaches in its TV commercials. The pressure came not from relatives of the departed insects, but Veterans groups who argued that the use of the tune demeaned the memory of servicemen who had died in combat.

A GEOGRAPHY LESSON FROM DANNY QUAYLE

Hawaii has always been a very pivotal role in the Pacific. It is in the Pacific. It is part of the United States that is an island that is right here.
> —Our favorite VP, visiting Hawaii

4

WHAT A WAY
TO GO

SNOWMOBILE DRIVER-OF-THE-YEAR AWARD . . .

Will probably not be posthumously awarded to Donald
Anderson, who was killed when he smashed his snowmobile
into a bison in Yellowstone National Park, the first snow-
mobile-animal collision in national park records.

MUSIC LOVERS, BEWARE!

Clifford Mangum, 17, of MacArthur, West Virginia, died of
electric shock when he deposited a coin in a jukebox after
emerging from a swim in a lake.

HOSPITAL PATIENTS, BEWARE!

Anthony Craddock, 5, was killed when his electrically op-
erated bed in Harlem Hospital in New York City suddenly

closed up, strangling him. To add insult to injury, the hospital first listed the cause of death as AIDS-related pneumonia.

BURGLARS, BEWARE!

Gregg Moore, 25, of Skiatook, Oklahoma, apparently burglarized a house to steal sports equipment. That turned out to be a fatal blunder. Moore stumbled down the stairs, then fell on a hunting arrow he was carrying, killing himself.

DUMMIES, BEWARE!

Cecil Carpenter, 54, of Richmond, Indiana, collapsed and died at the National Ventriloquists' Convention. He was buried a few days later in a coffin with Alex, his dummy of ten years.

DOUBLE WHAMMY

Evangelista Denigris of Queens, New York, was on his way home from work one night when he lost control of his car, which flipped upside-down on a major parkway. Miraculously, Denigris survived. He somehow managed to crawl out of the wreckage—then was killed when a hit-and-run driver smashed into him.

KITTY LITTER

A 16-month-old boy in Cheraw, South Carolina, was mauled to death by a leopard while strapped into his car seat. The animal had escaped from a pen on a farm owned by the boy's parents, and had attacked the tot while his grandmother was taking packages into the house. The farm was home to twelve lions and other big cats, which the boy's parents displayed at fairs and malls throughout the Southeast.

OLD FOLKS, BEWARE!

A 79-year-old resident who wandered away from a Benton, Arkansas, nursing home was found strangled to death by barbed wire six days later.

MOST AWFUL STORY OF THE YEAR

An Arvada, California, mother hit a line drive during a family baseball game that struck her 6-year-old son in the chest, killing him.

REMEMBER, PEDESTRIANS HAVE THE RIGHT OF WAY

You have to be *very* careful driving in New York. Frederick Stager of Brooklyn learned the hard way. He was forced to stop his car when a pedestrian blocked his way by standing in the middle of the street. Stager honked his horn; the pedestrian pulled out a gun and shot him dead.

JUNIOR? OH, HE'S IN THE YARD

A 68-year-old woman walked into a Troy, New York, police station and confessed that she had murdered her newborn baby thirty-eight years previously. The woman led police to the grave site, a spot in her backyard that she'd looked at from her kitchen window for almost four decades. The woman's husband never knew of the baby's existence or death, and wasn't charged.

WELL, THEY WEREN'T MUGGED

Two Philadelphia sisters drove to New York for a shopping spree. The older sister, nervous about crime in the Big Apple, brought along an antique German revolver for protection. During their visit, the girls stopped into a bar to use the bathroom. The older sister gave the weapon to her sibling before using the facilities. When she came back to the table, she reached to take the revolver. It discharged and a bullet entered the younger sister's head below the right eye, killing her.

POACHER OF THE YEAR

A Muskegon, Michigan, religious fundamentalist was convicted of murder for killing his 2-year-old and 15-month-old sons by boiling them in a foundry ladle.

COP WAS DUMB, NOW HE'S DEAD

A young New York City policeman and his girlfriend allegedly got their kicks by playing real games of Russian roulette with one live round in the cop's service revolver. About 3 A.M. one morning, the girlfriend saw the revolver lying on a table. Thinking the gun was empty, she picked it up, pointed it at the cop, playfully asked, "Are we playing this game?" and pulled the trigger. The gun was loaded and a bullet entered the cop's head above the right eye, killing him instantly.

SIBLING RIVALRY

A 14-month-old girl was stabbed with a screwdriver and beaten with a hammer by two brothers, ages 4 and 5. One boy told police, "She was ugly; we liked doing it."

GRAMPS IS RAISING CANE AGAIN

An 88-year-old man from Dade City, Florida, evidently has great strength and vigor for a man his age. Unfortunately, those qualities proved tragic for other residents of the nursing home in which the man lived. According to police, the codger was upset over "interpersonal problems among the male and female patients." So he allegedly got out of bed one night, grabbed his cane, beat to death two patients, and bludgeoned four others.

PARTY ANIMALS, BEWARE!

Joe Rutherford of Memphis, Tennessee, had a few drinks while waiting to change planes in St. Louis. Evidently bored, the man spotted an electric cart, got in, and started racing through the airport. His antics caught the attention of the cops, who gave chase. Then Rutherford made a mistake—he decided to hide in a trash compactor. A few minutes later, there wasn't enough left of him to fit in a carry-on bag.

MAN KILLED BY TOOTHPICK

The New England Journal of Medicine reported that an autopsy revealed that a California man died of complications caused by swallowing a toothpick six months earlier. The toothpick had lodged in an abdominal artery, causing fever, chills, and bleeding.

The journal also reported that toothpicks had caused 8,176 serious injuries over a four-year period, including three other deaths.

THE LEADING PARENT-OF-THE-YEAR AWARD CANDIDATES

A Lakeland, Florida, couple were charged with first-degree murder after they killed their 2-year-old son by dunking his head in the toilet because they had trouble potty-training him.

UNLUCKIEST BURGLAR

The cardinal rule of burglary is to get in, get the loot, and get out fast. That rule was broken by a burglar in Los Angeles, who stayed around to eat a sandwich and watch a little TV. Unfortunately, the house had just been fumigated with toxic fumes, which killed him.

OOPS

Minneapolis police suspended their practice of throwing flash grenades into a room to distract suspects after a grenade set a fire that killed an innocent elderly couple.

SHE FLICKED HER BIC

A 57-year-old Manhattan man was killed when his 29-year-old female companion whipped out a Bic pen and stabbed him in the heart.

OBESITY CAN BE DANGEROUS TO YOUR HEALTH

A 47-year-old Connecticut man was killed when his 500-pound wife fell on him during an argument. The man allegedly had called her a "fat-ass ox." So she allegedly fell on her 170-pound husband, beat him with her shoe, had her son tie the man's hands, then sat on him until police arrived.

WHILE YOU'RE WAITING, WOULD YOU LIKE SOME MORE JUICE?

No matter how you feel about the death penalty, you have to admit it was cruel and unusual punishment when Alabama prison authorities strapped convicted killer Horace Dunkins in the chair, flipped the switch—and discovered a wiring error resulted in insufficient voltage to kill him. The mildly retarded prisoner had to sit, strapped in, for nineteen minutes, until the wiring was corrected and the juice was turned on for a second, and fatal, time.

TURN REGULARLY FOR EVEN TANNING

A 45-year-old Chicago woman who was taking medication that made her skin more sensitive to light was roasted to death during a session in a tanning booth.

5

AMONG THE
THINGS YOU DIDN'T
WANT TO KNOW

IN THE VITAL SCIENTIFIC RESEARCH DEPARTMENT

The Genessee County Humane Society in Michigan announced that it was launching a study to determine if hogs suffer undue stress during pig-wrestling contests.

CHECK THE SPICE CABINET BEFORE YOU GO TO BED

Italian authorities seized what remained of a shipment of oregano that was being exported to the rest of Europe and the United States after receiving reports that the spice glowed slightly in the dark. Turned out that the oregano had indeed been exposed to radiation.

FOR A GOOD TIME, CALL ROTO-ROOTER

One of the last sanctuaries of mankind is under attack, at least if a new Phoenix, Arizona, company becomes successful.

In-Stall Ad Systems has begun mounting framed advertisements on the back of each stall door in public restrooms.

OUR FAVORITE NEW MUSEUM OF THE YEAR . . .

. . . is the Bra Museum in Stamford, Connecticut. The curator, who happens to be tatoo artist Spider Webb, has collected garments made during the entire century, including a tinfoil bra, a Plexiglas bra, and a cockroach bra. No doubt he'll next be contacting Dolly Parton to ask for her support.

ATTACK, MUFFIN!

We've heard of bleeding-heart liberals, but the Berkeley, California, city council must have set a new record for wimpish nonsense when the police department requested funds to purchase a trained dog to combat a rapidly escalating drug problem. The council agreed to go along with the purchase, but added the stipulation that the cops couldn't purchase a German shepherd or other breed of large dog normally trained to do that work. The council declared that the sight of a large dog might frighten citizens (drug dealers, for example). So the police department has spent months in a fruitless search for a harmless little drug sniffer? If you have a poodle that can recognize cocaine, you might want to give the Berkeley police department a call.

ENTERTAINING ASSES

A Broome County, New York, superior court judge denied a petition from the Humane Society to halt a circus act in which mules dived into a pool from a thirty-foot platform. Things must really be dull in Broome County.

WE ALL MAKE MISTAKES

Doctors were extremely embarrassed when a premature baby who'd been pronounced dead began crying—just as a funeral home worker arrived to pick up the body.

FAR FROM PAINLESS DENTISTRY

A dental hygienist in Grand Rapids, Michigan, was fired from her job because she preached to helpless patients while she was working on their teeth. The only thing worse we could imagine was having a hygienist who sold insurance on the side.

GREAT MOMENTS IN MEDICINE

Is your doctor being honest and upright in his dealings with you? Not if the editor of *Medical Economics* magazine has his way. You see, *Medical Economics* contains articles that deal with malpractice, setting fees, self-policing of the profession, and other matters related to billing and ethics. In a 1989 "Memo from the Editor," the editor of the publication cautioned readers that his magazine, "isn't made available to the general public. And we work hard at keeping it that way."

He went on to tell physicians, "You can do your part by restricting access to your personal copies of the magazine. Don't put them in the waiting room, don't leave them lying about in examining rooms, and don't abandon them in public places." God forbid we should understand how a doctor computes his bills.

WHERE'S THE KITTY?

The *Wall Street Journal* reported that unclaimed stray pets in the New York City Society for the Prevention of Cruelty to Animals shelter are destroyed, then collected by a rendering company. The pets are then "boiled down to by-products used in cosmetics and other products." The article said a kitten could wind up as "a bar of soap."

HOT GOSSIP FROM THE MIDDLE AGES

King Henry VIII of England was famous for, among other things, carving off the heads of a couple of his wives. In a discovery that smacks a little of poetic justice, historians now believe Henry's passion for carving meat probably killed him. In the September 1989 issue of *History Today*, an article claimed that the monarch ate so much meat and so few fruits and vegetables that he died of scurvy, a disease caused by a deficiency of vitamin C.

THE MOST APPROPRIATE MUNICIPAL GOVERNMENT DECISION OF THE YEAR

The city government of Chicago, Illinois, announced that arrangements had been made to take all old memos and other waste paper and recycle them into toilet paper.

A MAN-BITES-DOG STORY

A group of schoolchildren frolicking in the waters of Long Island Sound were attacked and bitten by a vicious school of bluefish. Two of the children needed more than twenty stitches after the onslaught of the game fish, which, in the words of a marine biologist, "have jaws structured like the piranha and sharp teeth like the barracuda." Rumor has it the bluefish were fleeing southward from the lures of President Bush, who was unsuccessfully fishing off the shores of Kennebunkport, Maine, at the time.

OUR SMALLEST (AND STUPIDEST) STATE

The tax division of the state of Rhode Island ruled that witchcraft is a legitimate religion and that covens are entitled to the same tax breaks as more established religions. If you're looking for a tax shelter, could we interest you in our tooth fairy cult?

HERE COMES "BAT MA'AM"

Evidently inspired by the hit movie, 36-year-old Vicki Graswich of Austin, Texas, began donning black tights, black knee-high boots, and a black cape to patrol her neighborhood after dark. Her target—rowdy teenagers who were breaking curfew. According to an Associated Press report, Bat Ma'am is usually successful in getting the kids to go home. No doubt the sight of her sets adults on the move, too.

GOD, THAT'S A LOT OF MONEY!

A study by the North American Securities Administrators Association and the Council of Better Business Bureaus revealed that Americans had been bilked out of $450 million in the last five years in religiously oriented swindles. The con artists ranged from "born again" financial planners who claimed God blessed their investments to an oil exploration firm that planned to drill in locations derived from the Old Testament.

BETTER BRUSH WITH PERRIER . . .

. . . at least if you're in San Francisco. The reason: The deputy manager of the Water Department reported that the city's watershed is teeming with wild pigs that frolic in the drinking water. Among the concerns are the fear that the wild swine could spread livestock diseases such as cholera.

WE DELIVER FOR YOU

Ever wonder where that lost package is? When New York Congressman Gary Ackerman was touring a mail-handling facility at Kennedy Airport, he got down on his hands and knees, reached under a conveyor belt, and pulled out dozens of two- to five-month-old packages that had fallen to the floor.

THE MARKETING IDEA OF THE YEAR . . .

. . . was revealed when Trojan announced a new "extra-strength" condom described as 25 percent stronger than anything else on the market. Tell us, can you think of a guy who would admit he didn't need an extra-strength condom?

GREAT MOMENTS IN EDUCATIONAL MOTIVATION

After his students at St. John Elementary School in Kansas had met his challenge to read more than a thousand books in four weeks, Principal Klon Mathews climbed up on the school roof and kissed a pig.

SPORTS UPDATE

Dwarf tossing, a favorite Australian pastime that involves heaving a small person across a barroom, has reached New Jersey. We've alerted the Environmental Protection Agency.

MUST SEE

Want to see the real Washington, D.C.? Then take a bus tour of the Washington Hall of Shame, which includes a stop at the townhouse where Gary Hart took Donna Rice, the area of the Tidal Basin where Wilbur Mills was stopped for drunk driving, and the spot on the Capitol steps where John Jenrette and his wife, Rita, allegedly made love. An added bonus—as a souvenir, tour members get a handful of "authentic" replicas of the documents Ollie North shredded.

SOLDIER, HIT THE DIRT AND GIVE ME A 1

The U.S. Army announced that new recruits were in such horrible physical condition that they've ordered drill sergeants to drastically reduce the amount and intensity of physical conditioning until the couch potatoes were in better shape. We are unable to print a single comment on this action by any of the nation's drill sergeants.

TRY THIS ONE ON YOUR BOSS

A veteran Lawrence, Massachusetts, policeman sued the town, arguing that being confined to a police cruiser had begun to make him "anxious and nauseated," a problem he called "a sort of cruiser syndrome." The cop sought three years' back pay and a permanent disability pension.

THEN THEY HID IT IN THE COMPACTOR

A crystal scientific test that survived blasting off into space, five days in orbit on the shuttle *Discovery*, and the rigors of re-entry into Earth's atmosphere was destroyed while going through an X-ray machine at Los Angeles Airport. And you wonder why your luggage gets so beat up.

HAPPY BIRTHDAY, GEORGE . . . LOVE, DAN AND MARILYN

Ready for the perfect gift for a terrorist who has everything? It's the new board game, "Save the President," in which the goal of some players is to assassinate our chief executive.

IN THE HUMANITARIANS-OF-THE-YEAR DEPARTMENT . . .

. . . are the bar owners in Atlanta, Georgia, who serve gigantic "last call" cocktails that cost $21 and contain as much as 46 ounces. Last call in Georgia is 3:55 A.M. on weekdays and 2:55 A.M. on weekends, so the people who order these have had a chance to get well-oiled already. After blasting themselves into orbit, some of these patrons go out and get into their cars.

EMPLOYMENT SECTION

The Census Bureau reported that in 1989 the number of elected politicians in the United States surpassed the number of bank tellers for the first time. Why the comparison? Both spend a large part of their day with their hands in the till.

FUN FOR THE WHOLE FAMILY

BE1 Defense Systems of Dallas, Texas, is advertising its "extraordinarily lethal" Flechette rockets with scratch-and-sniff ads that allow arms buyers to get a whiff of the aroma of cordite, the smell that follows a rocket explosion.

MICKEY, BEWARE!

A fire in a Maine laboratory killed 500,000 mice, causing a severe rodent shortage in laboratories across the country.

IN THE GOOD TASTE DEPARTMENT

The honors go to the vendors outside the prison where mass murderer Ted Bundy was electrocuted. Among the T-shirts for sale:
"Buckle up Bundy. It's the law."
"Hi ho, hi ho, it's off to hell we go."
"Bundy BBQ"

STAND-UP GUYS

Ever wonder why the line outside the ladies' room is so much longer than the line outside the men's room? A Cornell University study ("Your Tuition Dollars in Action") showed that women spend an average of seventy-nine seconds in a bathroom stall, compared with just forty-five seconds for men.

NEW PRODUCT OF THE YEAR

It's a concoction of a Bradley University student that's named Essence of Peoria, a substance that emulates the stink of the ethanol plants of that city. Its manufacturer described it as "the smell of very old beer—kind of an egg-sulfur smell." No doubt this potion will soon be joined by Essence of Jersey City, Essence of Gary, and other new fragrances.

AT LEAST HE SHOULD SAY EXCUSE ME

The New Hampshire State Supreme Court was asked to determine when a belch was intentional. This bizarre appeal stemmed from the arrest of an allegedly drunk driver. Police contend that the man deliberately belched every time they tried to take a Breathalyzer test in order to ruin the results. The man's attorney argues that there is no logical way to prove the belches weren't accidental. Don't hold your breath for the results.

LET THE CHIPS FALL WHERE THEY MAY

Gambling folks headed for the Schaghticoke Fair near Albany, New York, to wager on America's newest game: Bossy Bingo. Here are the rules. Players pay $5 for a numbered square on a 200' × 170' fenced-in field. Then three cows are let loose on the field. The owner of any square on which a cow stops and plops is the winner. Rumor has it the sport has a new publication, *Meadow Muffin News.*

SEND THAT SHYSTER TO REFORM SCHOOL!

The State of New York has proposed establishing a "reform school" to rehabilitate lawyers, doctors, and other professionals guilty of unethical or corrupt conduct. One potential problem: finding a facility large enough.

IN THE DEPRESSING NEWS DEPARTMENT

One out of every seventy-seven women who gave birth in New York City last year was infected with AIDS.

"OUR READING TODAY IS FROM THE FIRST BOOK OF TROJAN . . ."

The city council of Berkeley, California, proposed legislation that would require hotels to place safe-sex kits, including condoms, next to the Bible in every room. The bill proposed that the kits would include a sign that read, "The Bible may save your soul, but this will save your life." Some hotel owners were appalled—including some who were worried that the hotel could be sued if a condom broke.

BLACK LIKE ME

Two firefighters in Boston, twin brothers, were suspended for allegedly misrepresenting their race on employment applications. The two had listed their race as white when they failed to make the department in 1975. Two years later, they applied again, listing their race as black, explaining their mother recently told them that their maternal great-grand-mother had been black. The Boston City Council wasn't impressed when the situation came to light. Said a fire department spokesman, "They look like six-foot-two white guys, Irish guys."

ABOUT 80 MILLION MEN BREATHE A SIGH OF RELIEF

In a decision that has far-reaching implications for many Americans, the Georgia Court of Appeals ruled that being a jerk isn't against the law. A Georgia woman, a branch manager for a bank, had sued her employer and a co-worker on grounds that the co-worker's obnoxious comments and pranks drove her from her job. However, the court ruled that "tasteless and rude social conduct . . . is not actionable."

THE IRS—DRIPPING WITH SYMPATHY AS USUAL

The Internal Revenue Service, always ready with good news for us Americans, announced a new manual that laid out detailed plans for resuming the collection of taxes within thirty days after a nuclear attack. Isn't that a lovely thought— the haunted survivors of a tragedy that kills tens of millions of their countrymen find a tax man knocking on their shelter doors.

FOR ALL YOU VISITORS TO THE BIG APPLE

New York City has 3 percent of the country's population but records 18 percent of all American robberies—nearly 1 out of every 5 robberies that occur in the United States.

SIT UPON MY KNEE, SONNY BOY

Children at a Buffalo, New York, state psychiatric facility formed a secret club known as the "kissing club" or "toy club" in which youngsters age 5 to 12 forced new patients to have sex with them. A mother of an 11-year-old who had been "initiated" into the sex club was told by a staff member that the incident was only "childish sex play."

BUT WOULD YOU REALLY LIKE TO LIVE IN MILWAUKEE?

Believe it or not, jaywalking is a crime in New York City. Of the city's more than seven million residents, a total of thirty-one received tickets for the offense in 1989. Don't spend a lot of time feeling sorry for these unlucky few—the fine is a whopping $2. In contrast, ever-alert Milwaukee cops nailed three thousand jaywalkers, each of whom had to ante up $37.

ROBIN HUD

Leading the pack of thieves who looted the Department of Housing and Urban Development during the Reagan Administration was Marilyn Harrell, who told a Senate committee that she stole $5.5 million while acting as a private foreclosure agent. She said she took the money and gave it all to the poor.

THE ARMY'S NEW WAR

The U.S. Army reported that AIDS was the leading killer of servicemen last year, taking the lives of more than six hundred soldiers.

BUT WHEN SHE CAME OUT, THE CAVE WAS *STUNNING*

Italian interior decorator Stefania Follini survived 130 days in a sealed cave with no human contact in an experiment to discover the effects of isolation on the human body. Follini's period without any news of the outside world was second only to Ronald Reagan's eight years as president.

SOMETHING YOU INTUITIVELY KNEW ALREADY

Newsweek magazine reported that in airline pilot slang, passengers are referred to as "dogs."

IT REALLY WAS A GOOD BOOK

Two inmates in the Dorchester, Maryland, county jail escaped by jimmying their cell door with a Bible cover.

DATE TO REMEMBER

The year 1989 marked the twenty-first anniversary of the founding of the International Polka Association's Museum and Hall of Fame in Chicago.

WORST PET CRAZE OF THE YEAR

For six bucks, you can walk into a pet shop and emerge with a three-inch-long Madagascar Hissing Roach, a little devil who hisses like an aerosol can and will run up and down your arm and shoulder.

6

IF YOU THINK YOU'VE GOT TROUBLES

KIDS WILL BE KIDS

Lebanon, Pennsylvania, police were cruising through town one day when they noticed some grammar school kids had set up a roadside stand. Problem was, they weren't selling lemonade. These enterprising tots were playing drug dealers, peddling grass clippings as marijuana and sugar as cocaine. Lebanon police chief Bernie Reilly commented, "We just lost the war on drugs."

AT LEAST HE LEFT THE COWS ALONE

A Wisconsin dairy farmer was ordered by a county judge to pay child support for the offspring of a sexual relationship between his 12-year-old son and a 19-year-old woman.

MORE NEWS FROM NORTH DAKOTA

There were a lot of red faces at the White House after it was revealed that a tree transplanted from the White House grounds to the grounds of the North Dakota state capitol in Bismarck, as a gift from President George Bush, was infested with destructive gypsy moths. The discovery of the pests marked the first time gypsy moths have ever been found in North Dakota.

IRS SEIZES TEDDY BEAR

Or, at least, those infernal revenue agents sent a notice to Dustin Crowley demanding $48,000 in back taxes and threatening to seize his property. That was quite a shock to Crowley, a 5-year-old resident of Ogden, Utah. Fortunately, the tot and his family fought back, and the IRS finally admitted the letter was a mistake and withdrew the threat to the tot's toys.

ADDING INSULT TO INJURY

A Long Island, New York, woman was ordered by a judge to pay more than $100,000 in legal fees resulting from the defense of her husband—who was convicted of murdering her parents and teenage brother.

WHAT'S "WRONGFUL LIFE"?

The courts in Indianapolis, Indiana, allowed the guardians of a 3-year-old boy to proceed with a "wrongful life" suit against a nursing home. The guardians charged negligence in allowing a retarded resident to be raped by another retarded resident, producing a child with no natural parents capable of raising him. Suing the nursing home for support for the boy is understandable. But what's "wrongful life"? Does that mean the boy is suing because he was born?

OUCH!

A Buffalo, New York, man was awarded $450,000 after surgeons amputated his penis in the erroneous belief that it was cancerous.

AND THE COP WAS HOPPING MAD

Many people stopped for speeding give in to the temptation to let the cop have it verbally. Nebraska State Senator Ernie Chambers went one step further, although inadvertently—he ran over the foot of the State Trooper. A careless driving charge was added to the speeding ticket.

HOT PANTS WENT OUT OF FASHION
YEARS AGO, LEROY

Housesitting isn't a difficult task, but Leroy Wiggins of Colorado Springs, Colorado, made a real mess of it. Wiggins was repairing his car when, somehow, his pants caught on fire. He managed to wriggle out of the pants, which then ignited the house, causing $85,000 in damage and injuring five people.

CUDDLY PET TRICK OF THE YEAR

A Kansas City, Missouri, man was hospitalized after his fifteen-foot pet python wrapped around him and squeezed him until he lost consciousness. Kansas City Animal Control officials said they were uncertain if the snake was trying to harm or hug its owner.

SOME PEOPLE REALLY DO NEED TO DRINK

The Medical Examiner of Holyoke, Massachusetts, had pronounced 82-year-old Helen Francoeur dead, and was preparing to begin an autopsy. His plans were interrupted, however, when a funeral worker noticed the "corpse" had moved. Turns out Helen was suffering from dehydration, not death.

HOW BAD IS DRUG VIOLENCE?

Long Beach, California, school authorities approved funding for a ten-foot-high bullet-proof barrier alongside the Lindberg Junior High School yard to protect students and teachers from the frequent gunfire on the streets outside the school.

GOSH, WE'RE VERY SORRY

Mistakes are mistakes, but few are as horrible as a Veterans Affairs Department medical center in Ohio that erroneously told a Vietnam vet he had AIDS. Before the mistake was corrected twelve days later, the vet's fiancée left him, his employer fired him, and he was making plans to commit suicide.

THEY'LL GET YOU ONE WAY OR THE OTHER

A Long Island, New York, woman who went to prison for attempting to hire a hit man to kill her then-husband filed suit against him for failure to make monthly support payments. The woman's attorney argued that the fact that she tried to kill the man didn't relieve him of any obligation to support her. The ex-husband told reporters, "I'm flabbergasted."

CHECK IT OUT

We all should be able to afford the casual attitude toward money of Southwest Missouri State University librarian Billie Hurst, who neglected to cash $108,125.38 in paychecks over the course of a few years.

IF YOU THINK YOU'VE GOT BAD NEIGHBORS . . .

. . . consider the plight of a Point Reyes Station, California, woman. The area under her house turned out to be the favorite mating location for all the skunks in the nearby area.

Although animal experts trapped and removed skunks every night, more kept returning to combine odor with amore.

TALK ABOUT BAD DATES ...

A Waikiki, Hawaii, woman agreed to go out with a 23-year-old man she'd recently met. He showed up at her apartment, held scissors to her neck, raped her, robbed her, and threw her into a water-filled bathtub. Then he tossed a plugged-in electric hair dryer into the tub in an attempt to kill her.

IMAGINE HER SURPRISE

A woman was awarded $18,000 by a Minot, North Dakota, court for injuries suffered when a bull at an indoor rodeo threw its rider, jumped three 5.5-foot-high restraining fences, stampeded down a hall, burst into the ladies' room, and pinned her against a wall.

"DOCTOR, ALF'S ON THE OTHER LINE"

An Ottawa, Kansas, family physician became convinced that extraterrestrials cruise the galaxies in spaceships. The doctor further believed that many of these extraterrestrials are actually angels. The Kansas State Board of Healing Arts believed that the physician's license to practice medicine should be suspended until he sees a shrink.

INGRATE OF THE YEAR

Documentary filmmaker Errol Morris became obsessed with an obscure case in which a man named Randall Adams had been convicted and sentenced to death for shooting a Dallas police officer in 1976. In the process of making a film about the case, Morris uncovered new and convincing evidence that Adams was innocent. Eventually, an Appeals Court overturned the conviction and Adams was freed from death row—thanks solely to the efforts of Morris.

This being America, what did Adams do? He sued Morris to get a larger share of profits from book and film offers.

IF YOU THINK YOU'VE GOT BAD LUCK . . .

. . . listen to the story of Richard Batista of Queens, New York. He was looking for a new car, so he went to an auction of cars seized by the City of New York. He paid the city $2,400 for a Saab Turbo, then spent $9,000 refurbishing it. However, when Batista went to register the car, he discovered that it had been reported stolen a year earlier. The Motor Vehicles Bureau seized the car from Batista. Adding insult to injury, the city refused to return his $2,400, even though they'd sold him a stolen vehicle.

ACTOR FROWNS ON DIMPLE SURGERY

Television commercial actor Laurence Conroy sued a plastic surgeon for $5 million, claiming that the physician improperly removed his dimples during a facelift procedure. Conroy claimed that his Irish-American dimply smile was the key to his success, and that his income plummeted after the surgery.

BUT THEN HE FELL OFF A LADDER

Lynn Collins of Albertville, Alaska, lost his ability to speak when he was struck by a car at age 16 and suffered brain damage that left him in a coma for eleven weeks. For seventeen years, he communicated in sign language and by using a computer. Then he had another accident, a fall through a plate-glass window that led to transfusion of three pints of blood. As blood flowed from his wound, Collins turned to the paramedics—and began to speak.

HER HUSBAND WAS A STINKER

Many women who file for divorce attach the above label to their husbands, but one wife meant it literally. She told a judge that her husband "has stopped washing his upper body and has stopped changing his clothes, wearing them for weeks at a time.... The odor permeated the entire apartment, including the carpets and furniture." So a judge ordered the husband out of their studio apartment. He protested that his wife stank, too, from time to time. But he was still BO-oted.

THEN THEY WENT ON A RAMPAGE IN A BARNEVELD LADIES' ROOM

Michael and Paul Mieden of Barneveld, Wisconsin, sued a neighbor for $73,000, charging that the neighbor's two bulls scaled a fence and impregnated thirty-two young heifers. The brothers charged that the early pregnancy of many of the heifers, which are sort of "teenage cows," ruined their potential as milk producers.

A DOPE-Y SIGN

Sheriff Bob Vogel of Volusia County, Florida, wanted to find a way to catch some of the drug traffickers who transported cocaine and other substances northward along Interstate 95. So he posted a warning sign on the highway: NARCOTICS INSPECTION AHEAD.

What's the catch? There is no inspection, but many panicked motorists made illegal U turns. Then the sheriff's men pulled them over and searched the cars.

MEANWHILE, BACK IN RHODE ISLAND

A judge in Johnston, Rhode Island, ordered a 33-year-old woman to pay a $500 fine every time her boyfriend stayed overnight. His reason: The boyfriend's presence isn't good for her three children. The American Civil Liberties Union, which is helping the woman file an appeal, says that courts have no jurisdiction over purely moral issues.

ANOTHER SIGN OF THE TIMES

A 12-year-old girl brought her can of mace to "Show and Tell," then accidentally sprayed herself and two friends, sending all of them to the hospital.

DID THE EARTH MOVE FOR YOU?

James Steurer, 79, was sitting on his bed one morning, tying his shoes, when there was a gas explosion in the basement. Steurer and his mattress were sent sailing up off the floor, through a massive hole in the wall, across the lawn, and onto the driveway, where they landed safely.

MISCARRIAGE OF JUSTICE

A Virginia physician who set up practice as a fertility specialist has been sued for several million dollars by couples who charge that he falsely told the women they were pregnant, then gave them hormone shots to give them the symptoms of pregnancy. The women charge that the physician gave them ultrasound tests and pointed out images on the screen that he said were the fetus. After collecting fees for a few months, the doctor would allegedly inform the women that they weren't pregnant after all. Most of the couples suing the doctor had been trying to have babies for a number of years.

THE MOST EXPENSIVE VIDEO RELEASE
OF THE YEAR . . .

. . . was a home video of a University of Texas student having sex with his girlfriend. When they broke up, he showed it to at least ten friends. She sued. A jury awarded her a million dollars.

THE BAR EXAM WAS A DRAG

A Los Angeles man was extremely upset when he failed the state bar exam. So he allegedly coerced his seven-months' pregnant wife to dress in men's clothing and take the bar exam again under his name. She took the test, did well enough to achieve the ninth highest score in the state, then went immediately to the hospital to give birth to her premature daughter. The man thereupon abandoned his wife and infant daughter. Adding insult to injury, the California State Supreme Court is taking action to disbar the wife for her role in the charade.

UNLUCKIEST MAN OF THE YEAR

A Connecticut man was infected with the AIDS virus in a bus crash in Africa. The man was on vacation when the bus he was riding careened over an embankment. The man was wounded by flying glass and infected when the blood of other victims spattered onto those wounds.

YOUNG LOVE

A 15-year-old West Palm Beach, Florida, girl who was stood up on prom night filed a lawsuit against her no-show date. The damages: $49.53 for her shoes, flowers, and hairdo. Although the defendant argued that he'd canceled the date because he broke his ankle, he anteed up the sum.

AH, THE SMELL OF IT!

Everyone, sooner or later, encounters those most vicious of indoor pests, the aerosol perfume demonstrator, who insists on dousing every passerby with whatever scent is being peddled. In 1989, an angry victim fought back by suing Bloomingdale's for $15 million, claiming a squirt of perfume triggered an allergic reaction that resulted in a hospital stay of eleven days and medical bills of $12,000.

7

SCANDAL AROUND
THE WORLD

BEIRUT, LEBANON

Lebanese officials have announced yet another crisis in the
war-torn city: Beirut's cemeteries are totally filled and there's
no place to put the dead. More than 150,000 people have been
killed in the Lebanese capital since 1975. The only alterna-
tives mentioned by officials are leaving the dead out in the
open or hauling them out of town to a distant location.
Apparently, no one's considered the logical alternative—stop
producing so many corpses.

SINGAPORE

The government of this small but prosperous Asian state
announced a crackdown on one of the most flagrant of international crimes—failure to flush a public toilet after finishing
one's business. A seventeen-man "Loo Patrol" is now prowl-
ing Singapore potties to apprehend wastrels, who are subject

to a $500 fine. The government announced it was also investigating means of electronic surveillance to enforce the law.

SCHAGEN, THE NETHERLANDS

A Korean War veteran became incensed when he saw the skeletal remains of a World War I British soldier on display in a Dutch museum. So the former commando enlisted the support of three friends and kidnapped the remains so that the soldier could get a "proper and honorable burial." The British Embassy assured the man that the soldier's remains would be buried.

LONDON, ENGLAND

London police wished they could turn to Sherlock Holmes after an unsuccessful search for the culprit who killed a pedestrian by throwing a turnip at him from a passing car. Also hospitalized was another man who suffered severe stomach injuries after being hit by a cabbage. Word is that the bobbies have staked out all stands selling rutabagas.

WEST GERMANY

Neo-Nazi groups are "infecting" electronic bulletin boards with more than twenty computer games like "Cleaning Up Germany," in which players score points by killing Jews, Turks, homosexuals, and environmentalists. Although the games are illegal, they are being spread through exchange of computer discs as well as through computer networks.

U.S.S.R.

Aeroflot Airlines: YOU HAVE MADE THE RIGHT CHOICE
—Advertising slogan for the Soviet
Union's only airline

TEHERAN, IRAN

The Ayatollah Khomeini was evidently extremely senile before his death. What other reason could he have sent a message to Soviet president Mikhail Gorbachev urging him to study Muslim ideology as a replacement for Communism. The aging madman wrote, "I expressly declare that the Islamic Republic of Iran, as the greatest and most powerful base in the world of Islam, can easily fill the ideological vacuum of your regime."

ROME, ITALY

In the most embarrassing Italian robbery of the year, thieves broke into the offices of a company and stole $25,000 in cash. What was so embarrassing? The company makes safes and burglar-proof doors.

HAVANA, CUBA

We all know asses who drink too much, but few of them put away thirty quarts a day, the average consumption of Pancho, a 30-year-old Cuban burro. Unfortunately, the booze caught up with the burro, bringing on a liver ailment. Vets cut the poor nag back to a mere ten quarts.

MONROVIA, LIBERIA

The Defense Minister of Liberia, his wife, and seven other people were accused of killing a young policeman, then using his heart and other organs in a black-magic ritual.

BRUSSELS, BELGIUM

The pilot of a Soviet bomber flying over Poland reported serious mechanical problems. Then he bailed out of the plane.

Evidently, those problems weren't as serious as he believed, because the Soviet plane flew 500 miles without a pilot, crossing several national borders before running out of fuel and crashing into a house in Belgium.

PRETORIA, SOUTH AFRICA

In a case that drew international attention, a South African court sentenced a white ex-policeman to death for killing seven blacks and an Indian man in order to start a race war. Although white extremists urged that the killer be freed, the court was horrified by the cold-blooded and unfeeling manner in which the killings were carried out. The defendant admitted that he'd been smiling while murdering the blacks, stating, "I'm a friendly person."

LONDON, ENGLAND

As part of a promotion to herald the release on videotape of a new horror film, producers mailed live snakes to video rental shop owners in London. Most shop owners thought that was a slimy thing to do, so the producers had to go around and collect the reptiles.

WARSAW, POLAND

Even his mother can't pronounce his name properly, and you'll have to get used to it.
> —Chief Polish government spokesman
> Jerzy Urban, introducing reporters to
> his successor, Zbyslaw Rykowski

MOSCOW, U.S.S.R.

The Soviet Union's first beauty queen, 17-year-old Yulia Sukhanova, charged that the thrill of being crowned Miss

U.S.S.R. has been ruined by threats and blackmail. Among her important charges were that the director of the pageant refused to let her travel with a chaperone so he could be alone with her. See, the commies can be letches, too.

LONDON, ENGLAND

The latest celebrity on the London medical scene isn't a physician, but a pooch—a 2-year-old dog named Baby, to be exact. Doctors are intrigued by reports that Baby, over the course of months, pointed to and tried to bite off a malignant tumor on her owner's thigh, while ignoring many other similar-looking moles. Rumor has it that it now takes three months to get an appointment with Baby.

RAVENNA, ITALY

Salman Rushdie wasn't the only author who incensed Islamic fanatics last year. Evidently, the Ayatollah's legions ran out of living people to threaten, so they turned on the great Italian poet Dante, who passed away 568 years ago. The reason for the anger—in his masterpiece, *The Divine Comedy*, Dante portrayed the prophet Mohammed as suffering in Hell. Italian police doubled the guard at Dante's tomb after repeated bomb threats.

SEOUL, SOUTH KOREA

The entire nation was shocked when four South Korean sisters, ages 6 to 13, ingested rat poison in a suicide pact designed to allow their parents to spend all of their money on the education of their brother, a 3-year-old. This story dramatizes the old-fashioned Korean attitude that values only male offspring. Fortunately, three of the four girls survived, and those girls were inundated with gifts and pledges of money.

CHANDIGARH, INDIA

They love their buffalos in India—maybe more than their wives. So when a buffalo swallowed $2,000 in jewelry owned by the wife of a farmer in this poor rural area, the man refused to kill the animal to recover the jewelry. Instead, he patiently waited twelve years until the animal died a natural death. No report of what his wife thought of the delay . . . or how soon she started wearing her jewelry again.

PARIS, FRANCE

The French company Michelin, producer of the famous Michelin guides and maps, came under fire from Jewish groups for issuing a map of northeast Africa and the Middle East that completely omitted Israel. The map showed Egypt and Jordan having a common border. A larger map avoids the issue by covering the portion occupied by Israel with an insert showing the entire continent of Africa. Jewish groups charge that the outrage stems from Michelin's reluctance to offend high-spending Arab customers.

JERUSALEM, ISRAEL

Soldiers mistook a Palestinian mayor's bodyguard for a terrorist and shot him to death.

HAVERFORDWEST, WALES

Chef Albert Grabham cooked the most expensive dinner in town on New Year's Day—his profits from New Year's Eve. He'd placed the money in the oven of his restaurant for safekeeping the night before—and forgot about it the next morning.

CHATHAM, ENGLAND

The hold that Marilyn Monroe has over the public world-wide, despite her death twenty-seven years ago, was chillingly demonstrated when a British model who made nearly $100,000 per year impersonating Monroe committed suicide in circumstances nearly identical to those of Monroe's death. Kay Kent, 24, was found lying dead on her bed, sleeping tablets scattered near her body. The bed was littered with photographs of Monroe, and other photographs of the actress, books, and voice recordings were stacked in the room.

8

THE MOST BIZARRE
SCANDALS OF 1989

SICKEST CASE OF THE YEAR

An Ossining, New York, computer expert was arrested on
209 counts of alleged sexual torture and abuse of boys, ages 7
to 17. The indictments charge that the man's crimes included
using a twelve-volt car battery to apply electric shocks to
victims' genitals. Police also alleged that the man would wrap
the boys' genitals with duct tape, then rip it off while he tape-
recorded their screams.

THE MOST BIZARRE NEW DRUG CRAZE OF 1989

As if the crack epidemic wasn't bad enough, we've now got
a new craze that's beginning to spread on the West Coast. The
new addiction: toad licking. Yes, we're serious. It seems that
certain varieties of toad, notably a species called the Sonoran
Desert, produces a chemical that seeps through the skin to
drive off predators. When licked off the toad or boiled out in
toad tea, the chemical produces a high.

Unfortunately, in larger quantities, the chemical can be fatal. If you're thinking of trying this disgusting habit, don't try to get through Customs with a toad in your pocket—possession of the chemical has been illegal since 1970.

TALK ABOUT RUINING A PARTY

The highlight of a St. Patrick's Day party in ritzy Malibu, California, was a singer delivered in a helicopter. In the midst of the festivities, the chopper landed and Chanel Price hopped out. As the crowd cheered, Price raised both hands in celebration—and the blades of the helicopter cut off the fingers on her left hand.

YET ANOTHER MOTHER OF THE YEAR

Police in Pocatello, Idaho, arrested a 23-year-old mother who allegedly put her baby daughter in a trash bag full of dirty cat litter and tossed the bag into the garbage.

GOD SAYS NO

Growing marijuana is so widespread that some growers have been heard bragging that their chances of getting caught are about the same as their chances of being struck by lightning. In that case, the odds caught up with a 47-year-old resident of Howard, Wisconsin. According to police, lightning started a fire in the man's home, igniting about eighty marijuana plants growing in the basement. Firefighters recognized the aroma and called in the cops.

TIP LEADS TO TOE MANIAC

When police raided the mobile home of a 57-year-old rural Pennsylvania man, they discovered the farmworker had an extremely odd fetish—feet and toes. A search of the man's house yielded hundreds of photographs of people's feet and films of marchers in parades with the camera zooming in on their feet. Most bizarre was the discovery of two big toes, two middle toes, and two little toes preserved in a glass jar.

Under questioning, the man admitted he'd cut one toe from the body of a 15-year-old hunting-accident victim by sneaking into the funeral home. The farmworker wouldn't say where he got the other toes. The alleged foot freak was arrested after a neighbor told police that the man proposed killing and mutilating a 17-year-old girl.

HISTORY LESSON OF THE YEAR

Scholars around the world no doubt keeled over in shock when insane Libyan dictator Colonel Muammar Qadaffi announced his conclusion that William Shakespeare was an Arab. Lived in Stratford-on-Nile, we hear.

FREE THE FETUS!

The Missouri state legislature passed an anti-abortion law that defined life as beginning at conception, stating that the unborn had "all the rights and immunities available to other persons." Taking that statement at face value, Jefferson City attorney Michael Box filed a federal lawsuit charging the state with unlawful imprisonment of a fetus. Box's pregnant client, Lovetta Farrar, was in jail after convictions for forgery and theft.

THE TRAGEDY OF HOMELESSNESS

The plight of the homeless was once again vividly portrayed by a report from Raleigh, North Carolina. The story began when a homeless man noticed people throwing peanuts to pigeons. The hungry man began to compete with the pigeons for the nuts. In his frenzy, he wrung the necks of pigeons who got to a nut before he did. Police were called, and the man was arrested for killing seven birds in an area designated as a bird sanctuary.

WHO GOT TO LICK THE ENVELOPES?

If you or I stuffed photos of naked people in envelopes and sent them through the mail, we'd have postal authorities on our tail. Not Senator Jesse Helms, the Senate's arch conservative and self-appointed arbiter of public taste. In an attempt to rally support to cut the budget of the National Endowment for the Arts, Helms sent copies of four photographs showing partial frontal nudity, all taken from a controversial exhibit, to other members of Congress. From what we've heard about Congress, Helms's technique was about as shocking as sending a copy of *National Geographic* to Hugh Hefner.

WAR IS SMELL!

Alleged odor caused a gigantic stink at the Seattle-Tacoma airport last June. An Iranian national and his American wife had just settled into their seats when a USAir employee asked them to leave the plane. When they got to the boarding ramp, the Iranian was told that his body odor was so strong that he couldn't take the flight. USAir employees gave him some deodorant to spray under his arms, but then decided that the smell was still too strong. The plane left without them.

The enraged couple threatened to sue, stating that they arrived at the airport clean and fresh as the morning dew. An airline spokesperson responded that the other passengers on the aircraft had applauded when the couple was escorted from the plane.

ANYTHING FOR A BUCK

It wasn't the shy or the squeamish who signed up for the "outrageous behavior" contests sponsored by radio stations in Huntsville and Birmingham, Alabama. The winners in both contests turned out to be Michael and Sonya Nau, who garnered $15,000 for diving into huge piles of fresh cow manure. That's bad enough—but how would you like to be the contestants who devoured mounds of worms . . . and lost?

LET'S SEE, WE'VE GOT THREE STEAKS, TWO CHOPS, LEG OF MOM . . .

A high school administrator in Detroit, Michigan, was arrested and charged with murder after his daughter found the body of her mother in the basement freezer.

SICK!

Oak Park, Illinois, authorities were investigating charges of racism in the police department, including allegations that some white officers amused themselves by placing a hangman's noose around the neck of a little lost black boy who came into the station.

COULDN'T HE JUST WATCH "SESAME STREET"?

His mother described the young lad as "a good boy." But that's hard to reconcile, considering what happened one day when the 9-year-old was home because school was closed due to a snowstorm. For an unexplained reason, he went to his father's gun cabinet, removed a hunting rifle, waited by the window, then fired at a 7-year-old girl riding on a snowmobile that passed by. Tragically, the girl died.

YET ANOTHER MOTHER-OF-THE-YEAR AWARD CANDIDATE

A 37-year-old Wyoming woman told police that she'd been receiving mysterious phone calls telling her that her children were replicas and that she'd have to kill them to get her real children back. So she allegedly beheaded her 15-month- and 4-month-old daughters.

BUT IT'S A STEP IN THE RIGHT DIRECTION

A Korean-born resident of Los Angeles, California, was accused of trying to rape a 23-year-old student. To make amends, the Korean allegedly cut off one of his fingers, gift-wrapped it in a box, and offered it to the girl as an apology. It didn't work.

OUR BUSY PROSECUTORS

In one of the year's most bizarre stories, the City Council of Auburn Hills, Michigan, issued a citation charging the Michigan state treasurer with scalping. The reason: Eight tickets to the NBA playoff game between the Detroit Pistons and the Los Angeles Lakers had been seized by police during a drug raid. In accordance with state policy, the tickets had been auctioned off with the other loot, bringing a bid of $2,804. The problem is that the tickets had a face value of only $200, meaning the state's sale violated anti-scalping laws. Is that clear?

THE CASE OF THE DEVOUT DORKS

Larry and Leona Cottam are Seventh Day Adventists, a religion that urges members to tithe 10 percent of their income to God. The Cottams ran out of money to buy food for themselves and their two children, Eric, 14, and Laura, 12. So they all decided to fast until the Lord came to their rescue. That decision, three weeks later, led to the starvation death of their son, Eric, whose 5'9" frame had wasted down to a mere 69 pounds.

When authorities entered the house, they discovered that

the Cottams had nearly $4,000 in cash. They told authorities that they had let their son starve to death rather than touch that money, which had been tithed to God. A jury convicted them on charges of third-degree murder.

THE POWER LUNCH

A gigantic colony of ants in Temple City, California, began munching on the wire insulation of street lights and traffic signals, causing short circuits and $22,000 in damage.

IF YOU'RE SQUEAMISH, MOVE ON TO THE NEXT ITEM OR GO FISHING

The New England Journal of Medicine reported that doctors removing an appendix were surprised when a two-inch-long worm suddenly wriggled into view, a worm that was the real cause of the man's pain. It apparently came from a piece of sushi, or raw fish, that the man had eaten the night before.

AS IF KILLER BEES WEREN'T BAD ENOUGH . . .

. . . now we have to worry about a new plague—meat-eating wasps. According to the California State Food and Agriculture Department, these wasps "will snatch a piece of chicken right out of your hands." These ferocious insects came from Europe, and they appear to be out for blood—they killed a horse that disturbed one of their nests. If you're heading west, you might want to forget about those picnic plans, unless you're a WASP yourself.

CHARLIE, WE ALL MISS YA

Two men in Tucson, Arizona, were arrested for taking all the possessions from the home of Charles Gill. Gill, however, didn't raise any objection—he'd been lying in his home dead for more than two years. According to police, absolutely no one missed him or knew he was dead. When the two men broke into the house, they found a mummified body, so they helped themselves. We can't help wondering—how did Gill's utility and other bills get paid?

ROSEANNE BARR COULD SAVE A CONTINENT

Chicago resident Dennis Genze, who lost 173 of his 430 pounds in six months, donated his excess skin to save burn victims.

BUT THAT'S HOW COLONEL SANDERS GOT HIS START

I would say certainly it violates the spirit, if not the letter, of the anti-cruelty law.
> —Humane Society executive, after learning that Lexington, Kentucky, was burying pigeons alive in its landfill

PERVERTED COLLECTORS ITEM

A Garland, Texas, gun dealer is asking $7,500 for the seven guns that mass murderer Charles Whitman used to kill sixteen people and wound thirty-one from the University of Texas Tower in 1966.

FUN GUY OF THE YEAR

A Malibu, California, man was allegedly driving a stolen pickup truck that crashed into a motorcycle, killing the driver. Shortly afterward, the man, totally nude, casually strolled into a restaurant, shouted a few "Hail Satans," then sat down at a table. The cops showed up to arrest him a few minutes later.

DOES KENTUCKY NEED SOME MORE LANDFILL?

A 16-year-old Brooklyn, New York, youth allegedly stabbed his mother in the throat because she wouldn't give him $200 to buy crack. Then, police say, he stripped her body to make it appear that she had been killed by a rapist. Shortly afterward, he was arrested, confessed, and was charged with the murder.

But the story doesn't end there. He was allowed, under heavy guard, to attend the funeral, where he read, "She taught me the best values in life. Sure, we had arguments, but doesn't every mother who wants the best for her son?" The answer is, yes—but every son doesn't stab his mother in the throat.

MOST HORRIFYING NEWS STORY OF THE 1980s

On January 20, 1989, Dan Quayle was probably the acting President of the United States between noon and shortly after 12:03 P.M., when George Bush was sworn in. Fortunately, the nation survived those harrowing 3.5 minutes.

TOO BAD, WE HAVE A FEW GALLBLADDERS FOR SALE

A woman in a Massachusetts town was fined $700 and sentenced to twenty-five hours of community service for purchasing bear gallbladders. She's an acupuncturist who uses them to treat hemorrhoids.

OUR HERO

A 36-year-old mailman had a very different hobby—collecting junk mail. He evidently was so obsessed by the stuff that he started bringing everyone else's junk mail home from his route. When authorities discovered this bizarre theft, they found 2.5 tons of the stuff in the man's home. Included were tens of thousands of sweepstakes entry forms, many sent by Ed McMahon.

THE YELLOW ROSE OF TEXAS

Police in North Richmond, Texas, thought they had a key piece of evidence when a witness told them that a female who had robbed a local service station had a rose tattooed on her left breast. To their astonishment, however, more than three hundred people from the small town called in to report that they knew a woman with that tattoo. Evidently, either the local tattoo parlors had been working overtime, or the robber was a very sociable lady.

HANDS DOWN, THE BAD-TASTE AWARD . . .

. . . goes to the art galleries in Boston, Chicago, Los Angeles, and Phoenix that have had formal showings of the artwork of John Wayne Gacy, the notorious mass murderer who was convicted in 1980 of the slayings of thirty-three boys and young men. One gallery owner regretted the showing, saying that "the people who came were suburban punks who thought serial killing was cool." A prison spokesman said that Gacy receives eight hundred letters a year. That is sick.

THE INSECT'S REVENGE

A 14-year-old Boulder, Colorado, boy was evidently very irritated by a bug on the porch of his home. So he doused the bug with insect repellent and set it on fire. The bug, however, had the last laugh. It flipped into the bushes and set them on fire. Then the bushes set the front porch on fire, the porch ignited the house wall, the wall ignited the roof, and then the roof ignited the second floor. All told, the bug did $40,000 in damage. Guess the kid should have used an old-fashioned swatter.

9

THE CELEBRITY
"SIN-DEX"

AGNEW, SPIRO: The former Vice President, apparently still unrepentant for taking bribes and other official misconduct, asked the California Board of Equalization to allow him to deduct from his taxes the restitution he had to pay the State of Maryland for taking bribes. That would mean, if approved, that the California taxpayers would pay part of Agnew's fine for being a crook.

BARRYMORE, DREW: The child star of *E.T.*, now 13, checked into an alcoholism treatment center. She revealed that she had begun drinking at age 8 and began using drugs at age 11. The Barrymore family has a history of heavy drinking.

BOESKY, IVAN: The Wall Street whiz convicted in a headline-making insider trading scam was evidently pouting when he arrived at Lompoc Federal Prison in California. Boesky refused to shower for his first ten days in jail, a stubbornness that created such a stink that his fellow inmates grabbed him, stripped him, and tossed him in the shower.

BOGDANOVICH, PETER: In one of the year's most bizarre love

stories, the 49-year-old director married 20-year-old Louise Hoogstratten, the younger sister of former Playmate of the Year Dorothy Stratten. Bogdanovich had been obsessed with Dorothy Stratten, who was brutally murdered by her husband in a fit of jealous rage in a story that was the subject of two feature films.

BROWN, JAMES: The godfather of soul, whose escapades resulted in a six-year prison sentence for aggravated assault, got into trouble again when prison guards found a whopping $40,600 in cash and checks in his cell. Prison rules prohibit a con from having more than $50.

BUSH, BARBARA: The usually gracious First Lady turned frosty when she lashed out at a *New York Times* reporter. Was it something written about her husband? Hardly. Instead, the subject was the famous First Puppies born to Millie, the First Dog. It seems that the puppy's box had been lined with shredded copies of the *Times*, but the ink rubbed off so easily that it turned the puppies gray. The First Family has reportedly switched to shredded *Washington Posts*.

DOWNEY, JR., MORTON: People who think the former talk-show host is crude can use evidence from a lawsuit filed against Downey by a New Jersey car-leasing firm. The firm maintained that in addition to owing $5,400 in back payments, Downey damaged his rental limousine by filling the crystal liquor decanters with urine, along with other debris.

DURAN, ROBERTO: The Panamanian fighter, several times world champion in different weight classes, was sued by the IRS. The reason: Instead of an expected $60,000 refund, the boxer received a total of $1.54 million in checks—which he spent. Unfortunately, the IRS caught on when Duran returned another uncashed check for $1.4 million.

EBERT, ROGER: A little-known fact about the famous film critic's life was that he penned the script for *Beyond the Valley of the Dolls*, a movie by erotic filmmaker Russ Meyers. The two met because both share a fascination with extremely large-breasted women.

FOX, MICHAEL J.: The TV and movie superstar's life became a nightmare when an avalanche of five thousand threatening letters and packages of rabbit droppings began to arrive. Fox's tormentor was a woman who evidently became enraged when the star married actress Tracy Pollan. When police failed to stop the harassment, Fox hired a private eye who nabbed the 26-year-old woman who had allegedly written the letters.

GILLESPIE, DIZZY: The famous jazz musician "left home without it"—his American Express card, as well as other identification. So American Express refused to replace his lost traveler's checks until Gillespie could prove who he was. He suggested American Express call his lawyer, Elliot Hoffman. Hoffman suggested, "Ask him what comes after 'oo-bop-sha-bam.' " When Gillespie replied, "alfoogle-mop," American Express issued the refund.

HAHN, JESSICA: As Jim Bakker had his day in court, the woman involved in the dalliance that precipitated his decline achieved yet another milestone in her fledgling show-business career. The one-time church secretary was hired to host "Thunder and Mud," a one-time-only cable show featuring heavy-metal bands and female mud-wrestling. Sounds irresistible.

HALL, FAWN: The loyal secretary to the self-proclaimed "super straight" Oliver North admitted that she used cocaine during a three-year period in which she had access to top secrets during her work at the National Security Council.

HAYES, ISAAC: The entertainer was jailed for being a whopping $346,300 behind in alimony and child-support payments.

HEFNER, HUGH: The king of the *Playboy* empire finally tied

the knot to Kimberley Conrad, a Playmate of the Year. Rumors swirled about how long it would be before Hefner's eyes roamed, but Conrad remarked, "I'm not worried that he will reject me. I'm 26. He's 62. Maybe I could reject him."

HILL, BENNY: The comedian who has become one of the two hundred richest people in Great Britain by playing a girl-chasing, sex-obsessed lecher on his television show is in reality an eccentric, celibate recluse, according to a new biography. Author John Smith says Hill spent a recent Christmas alone in his unheated house, watching television, and shaving with the same water he'd used to boil an egg.

HITLER, ADOLF: Over four decades after his suicide in a Berlin bunker, the Nazi maniac is still causing trouble. In 1989, Hitler's personal yacht was sunk in the Atlantic Ocean to commemorate the infamous "Voyage of the Damned," in which a ship filled with Jewish refugees seeking to escape from Hitler found no haven. The problem: For some inexplicable reason, the yacht was sunk in the wrong place, obstructing an important shipping lane off the coast of Miami, Florida.

HUMPERDINCK, ENGELBERT: The singer, in discussing plans for a forthcoming autobiography, revealed information that is certain to put him in the *Guinness Book of World Records*. Humperdinck made Steve Garvey look like a virgin by admitting that he's been the defendant in fifteen paternity suits.

JENRETTE, JOHN: The former Congressman, who made national headlines when he was convicted in the Abscam investigation in 1980, was headed back to the slammer on a thirty-day sentence for stealing a necktie and shoes from a discount store.

JOHNSON, DON: The star of "Miami Vice" made a real-life collar when he caught a thief rummaging through a hotel suite he was sharing with former and future wife Melanie

Griffith. Johnson quickly tackled the startled burglar, while Griffith called the police.

JONES, TOM: The heartthrob singer lost a paternity suit when blood tests revealed a 99.76 percent certainty that Jones was the father of Jonathan Jones Berkery.

KENNEDY, JOHN F.: The former President's philandering was vividly documented in a biography of his wife, Jackie, written by C. David Heymann. Among the stories:

- Kennedy and Senator Estes Kefauver once made love to their dates in front of other guests at a party in a hotel suite—then switched women and started again.
- Kennedy dashed to a hotel room for a tryst with Angie Dickinson during an Inaugural Ball, then later that evening had a ménage-à-trois with two Hollywood starlets.
- Kennedy had sex with a call girl minutes before his first debate with Richard Nixon.
- Kennedy hosted wild pool parties at the White House that quickly broke up when Jackie appeared.
- Kennedy's first meeting during any stop on a Presidential visit was with the Secret Service agent in charge of lining up women for him.

KENNEDY, TED: Twenty years later, a new round of publicity cast light on the Senator's alleged culpability in the drowning death of Mary Jo Kopechne when the car he was driving careened off the Chappaquiddick bridge. Most damaging was the report from a diver who recovered Kopechne's body. The diver said that he believed that the girl could have been rescued alive if Kennedy had summoned help promptly.

In yet another story involving the Massachusetts Senator and a woman, author Sharon Churcher charged, in an article in *Penthouse*, that Kennedy was pawing a waitress at Washington's fashionable La Brasserie restaurant. On another occasion, the article states, a waitress walked into a private room at the restaurant to find Kennedy having sex on the floor with a blonde. A Kennedy spokesman commented that the Senator was "entitled to his private life."

KISS: The bad-boy rock group was sued by owners of a forty-two-story New York City office building. The suit contends that the building was turned into a phallic symbol by the way it was photographed in a Kiss music video. We're not sure about the grounds of the suit—were the building's feelings hurt?

L.L. COOL J.: In yet another sordid story involving tours by rap groups, three members from the star rap musician's touring company were arrested in Minneapolis for allegedly raping a 15-year-old fan who had been lured to a hotel room. The teenager had won a pass to go backstage at L.L. Cool J.'s concert in a radio contest. The touring group's members who were arrested allegedly convinced the girl that she would meet L.L. Cool J. back at the hotel. L.L. Cool J. was not involved in the alleged assault.

LOWE, ROB: As part of an agreement, the DA agreed not to prosecute Lowe over his famous sex tapes and Lowe had to lecture in Los Angeles schools on the dangers of drugs. However, it turned out the Los Angeles School Board doesn't want any part of Lowe. Said the board president, "It appears on the surface he has, at minimum, dubious judgment."

After the much-publicized video sexcapades of the movie actor, jokes circulated that his next movie would be *Two Men and a Baby*. Truth is stranger than humor, however. As the sordid story hit the front pages, Lowe was filming a movie titled *Bad Influence*, the subject of which is a drifter who secretly videotapes a businessman having sex with a woman.

In an informal survey of Americans conducted by the Paragon Project, we discovered that a significant majority of you believe that Lowe's most obscene video of the year was the musical number he did with Snow White on the Oscar telecast. Experts have labeled the opening number as the most embarrassing in Oscar history.

MADONNA: According to numerous press reports, the famous entertainer spent her New Year's Eve "trussed up like a turkey" after being beaten, gagged, strapped to an armchair, and left alone for nine hours by her ex-husband, Sean Penn.

The superstar named her production company Siren Films, saying, "You know what a siren is? She's a woman who draws men to their death."

MOUSE, MICKEY: This little rodent is one of the most lovable creatures in the country. But painting his picture on the wall has brought the wrath of the giant Disney Company down on a small day-care center in Hallandale, Florida. Disney ordered the Very Important Babies Day Care to remove pictures of Mickey, Minnie, Goofy, and Donald Duck, or face a lawsuit. An overwhelming number of callers to the center thought Mickey's owners were rats for their harassment.

MURPHY, EDDIE: The comedian and actor was the target of a multimillion-dollar lawsuit filed by Michael Michele, a young actress hired to play a featured role in the movie *Harlem Nights*, which Murphy was going to direct as well as star in. The actress claimed she was fired because she refused Murphy's advances. His spokesman said there had been a personality clash. The courts will decide.

ONASSIS, CHRISTINA: New details of the tragic life of the fabulously wealthy heiress emerged in a biography by a London *Daily Mail* reporter. Among the revelations: Onassis was so obsessed with having a second child by her ex-husband Thierry Roussel that she bought him a $160,000 Ferrari Testarossa in exchange for making a deposit into a sperm bank. Another story: When a man she admired told her only blondes turned him on, she had her hair dyed blond—all over her body.

PAYCHECK, JOHNNY: The country singer was sentenced to nine and one-half years in jail for shooting a man in a barroom brawl.

PERDUE, FRANK: The poultry king evidently gets his kicks out of playing chicken with the law. The chairman of Perdue Farms admitted that he'd chalked up thirty-four convictions for traffic violations in twenty-one years. Curiously, Perdue never had his driver's license suspended.

PHILBIN, REGIS: The talk-show host, who earns an estimated $2 million per year hosting "Live with Regis and Kathie Lee," reportedly has a 26-year-old handicapped son who is struggling financially in Los Angeles. The son, who was born with deformed legs that had to be amputated, alleges that he is working to finish college despite his physical handicaps, financial problems, and the feeling that he's been abandoned by his wealthy father.

PRESLEY, LISA MARIE: The authors of *Elvis, My Dad: The Lisa Marie Presley Story* had a great deal of difficulty coming up with enough material to write a book about someone who hasn't accomplished anything, including graduating from high school. Said one co-author, "Both Elvis and Priscilla graduated from high school. Lisa couldn't manage that. She's not particularly alert."

PRINCESS ANNE: Britain's sometimes dowdy-looking royal was revealed to have a steamy secret life, at least according to headline stories in the British press. Early in the year came the release of love letters that were from a current secret romance. Just when that furor died down, the juiciest scandal came—reports that the father of Princess Anne's 8-year-old daughter, Zara, was not her husband, Mark Phillips, but a married detective who'd been assigned to guard her. The detective was fired by Scotland Yard for being "overfamiliar" shortly after the girl's birth. These stories were far from the first involving adulteries by the royal couple. So it was no surprise when Buckingham Palace announced that Princess Anne and Phillips had formally separated.

PRYOR, RICHARD: The movie star got burned again—this time by a blood test that indicated a 99.69 percent certainty that he was the father of a 2-year-old child. Pryor was stuck with a court order to pay $4,500 per month in child support.

REAGAN, MAUREEN: In her book, *First Father, First Daughter*, the daughter of former President Ronald Reagan and actress Jane Wyman revealed that she was brutally beaten by her first husband, a police officer. She detailed a horrifying series of physical beatings, including one occasion on which her husband came home drunk, strangled her until she fell to the floor, then kicked her in the head until she blacked out. The tragic episode in her life has made Reagan an outspoken advocate for the rights of battered women.

REAGAN, NANCY: One of the former First Lady's last official events was a mini "Just Say No" to drugs rally at Rockefeller Center in New York City. Mrs. Reagan had invited eighty-five schoolchildren to be bussed in to join her for snacks. However, fifty-five of the children went home bitterly disappointed after they were denied admission to the event by Secret Service agents because the room was too crowded. Somehow, however, Mrs. Reagan's people found the space for ten television crews. We guess the First Lady would rather say no to children than publicity.

REAGAN, RONALD: *American Spectator*, a conservative periodical, led a campaign to add Reagan's likeness to Mount Rushmore. The magazine said, "There is room for Reagan either to the right of Washington or between Roosevelt and Lincoln. The latter position . . . contains a large patch of rust-orange moss that could ideally serve as the president's hair." Needless to say, this campaign has picked up little public support.

RICE, DONNA: The stunning blonde, whose romp on a boat with Gary Hart sank his political ambitions, spent several weeks in 1989 at a religious retreat in Virginia. Rice reportedly told friends that she's "turned her life over to Christ." Good thing Jesus isn't running for President.

SCHAEFFER, REBECCA: This bright, beautiful, and talented 21-

year-old actress was brutally slain by a 19-year-old man who had become obsessed with her. Compounding the tragedy was the information that the killer had tracked Schaeffer down by obtaining her address through the California Department of Motor Vehicles. The shocking revelation cast light on a California law that allows anyone to obtain any driver's home address by filling out a form and paying a small fee.

SIMPSON, O.J.: The famous ex-football star and spokesperson for a major car rental firm was hauled into court for putting some "hurts" on his wife. His sentence included community service and counseling.

STEVENS, CAT: The former pop singer, who has changed his name to Yussif Islam, joined the Ayatollah Khomeini in calling for the death of author Salman Rushdie. Thereupon, millions of Americans called for a boycott of Stevens's songs and records.

TIFFANY: In a situation chillingly reminiscent of the tragic obsession that led to Rebecca Schaeffer's death, this teenage pop singer had to go to court to keep a fanatical fan away from her. Tiffany testified that the man had followed her for months, claiming that "God wants us together." The man allegedly threatened to cause her physical and emotional injury.

TIPTON, BILLY: After the death of the late, great jazz pianist, doctors revealed that Tipton was really a woman—a fact hidden from everyone, including his children, for more than forty years. Said his son after the incredible revelation, "Now I know why I couldn't get him to the doctor."

TRUMP, DONALD: The billionaire real estate tycoon bragged a little too much, and it cost him. The story: In his book *The Art of the Deal*, Trump bragged that purchasing his Palm Beach County, Florida, estate for $7 million was a steal. The county tax appraisers read the book and decided it was time for a real appraisal. They agreed with Trump and doubled the appraisal of the house to $14 million. That will cost Trump an additional $300,000 yearly in real estate taxes.

In what appeared to be yet another attempt to secure his hold on the title "America's Largest Ego," the New York billionaire filed suit against a small Georgia company that dared to call its line of business cards, "Trump Cards." Ignoring the small company's argument that "trump card" was a common English language expression, the mogul argued that he has exclusive rights to the word. We can't wait until Trump sues Disney to force the studio to rename its beloved character "Fred Duck."

TRUMP, IVANA: The wife of Donald also believes that she owns exclusive rights to her name—but in this case, it's her first name. She sued a Nyack, New York, cosmetics company for $10 million for marketing a lipstick called Ivana, claiming that she was so famous that she had exclusive rights to the name. Now, there's an injustice the American people can rally around.

TYSON, MIKE: A biography of the heavyweight champ by his longtime friend and New York State Boxing Commission Chairman José Torres portrayed him as a violent, chauvinistic man who liked to use his fists on women. Among the quotes in the book is Tyson's answer to the question, "What's the best punch you've ever thrown in your life?" According to Torres, Tyson replied, "Man, I'll never forget that punch. It was when I fought with Robin [Givens] in Steve's apartment. She really offended me and I went bam and she flew backward, hitting every fucking wall in the apartment. That was the best punch I've ever thrown in my fucking life."

WINFIELD, DAVE: The New York Yankees slugger was ruled a bigamist by a Texas jury that decided Winfield's relationship to Sandra Renfro, a former airline stewardess, constituted a common law marriage. That could mean that half of everything the slugger earned in those years could go to Renfro.

WINFREY, OPRAH: In one of the year's weirdest stories, *TV*

Guide admitted that it fitted the head of the talk-show hostess to the slinkily clad, lithe body of Ann-Margret for an August issue. There was little comment from Winfrey, who had to have been flattered. However, we hope this doesn't start a new trend—e.g., Warren Beatty's head on Arnold Schwarzenegger's body; Roseanne Barr's head on Dumbo's body . . .

WOODS, JAMES: The intense actor filed suit against actress Sean Young, his co-star and lover while the two were filming *The Boost.* Woods charges that Young harassed him and his present fiancée. The actor, referring to the situation, asked, "Does the word *nightmare* mean anything to you?"

WYMAN, BILL: The 52-year-old Rolling Stone finally wed Mandy Smith, 19. Wyman's romance with Smith made headlines when he started dating her at age 13. But this celebrity May-December marriage was only half a family affair—Wyman's 28-year-old son Stephen is dating Smith's 38-year-old mother, Patsy. That means that if Stephen and Patsy have a son, the kid will be Wyman's grandchild and his wife's brother.

10

AMERICA'S TEN GREEDIEST CORPORATIONS

In the past few years, it's been extremely difficult to tell the business pages from the crime reports. The only difference: Crooks on Wall Street and other business fronts steal not hundreds of dollars, but hundreds of millions of dollars. Corporate raiders, the new pirates, line their pockets with tens of millions of dollars while saddling corporations (and stockholders) with such monumental debt that thousands of employees have to lose their jobs. Other corporations devastate local communities by abruptly moving plants overseas or, even worse, polluting the environment so badly that rates of serious illness soar.

Of course, not all corporations are merciless and greedy. That makes it more important to point the finger every year at the worst of the worst. We at the Paragon Project have surveyed writers, environmentalists, and others who observe the corporate scene to develop the following Greediest List.

1. Exxon: The uncontested champion of 1989 and, if the Alaska cleanup continues at the present pace, a contender for the title in years to come. Exxon not only did a horrible job

cleaning up the disaster, it boldly boosted gasoline prices so that consumers footed the entire bill.

2. The Rest of the Oil Industry: Mobil, Texaco, Sunoco, and all the other members of this industry gleefully used the Exxon spill as an excuse to price-gouge the public. They all ought to be boiled in a few hundred gallons of crude.

3. McDonalds: Ronald McDonald and a host of lovable characters lure American children through the Golden Arches, where they purchase sandwiches in Styrofoam containers that are helping to rapidly destroy the ozone layer. McDonalds has announced a plan to gradually reduce the use of Styrofoam, though others believe the only moral action is to stop it now.

4. The Disney Company: Mickey Mouse may be the corporate logo, but the newly acquired Miss Piggy might more accurately reflect the corporate attitude of this giant that is setting about to corner the kiddie entertainment dollar. A one-day visit to Disney World already sets a family of four back $100 to get in the gates. Tens of thousands of tourists, attracted by a Disney campaign, flocked to the new MGM-Disney studios, only to find a plethora of long lines and a paucity of restaurants and attractions.

5. Eastern Airlines: The greed of airline executive Frank Lorenzo ruined the travel plans of millions of Americans, harmed the economies of cities served by the airline, and devastated the lives of thousands of hard-working, loyal employees. And for what? Lorenzo's companies are still on the verge of bankruptcy.

6. Drexel Burnham Lambert: The most notable of the Wall Street firms that garnered obscene fees from corporate takeovers and mergers. Any corporation that could pay a single executive over $100 million in one year while tens of thousands of children were homeless on city streets should become the target of congressional action.

7. Major League Baseball: Owners raked in gigantic payments from a new television contract. The price for the average fan: Baseball will virtually vanish from free network TV, robbing tens of millions of Americans without local teams or cable TV the opportunity to view the national pastime.

8. America's Coffee Companies: Have you noticed that most "one-pound cans" of coffee now contain a mere thirteen ounces? Coffee makers argue that new processing techniques give consumers the same amount of beverage despite the reduction in coffee. If anyone really believes that, please write us here at the Paragon Project.

9. Burroughs Wellcome Company: The patent holder of AZT, the only drug proven effective in lengthening the life of AIDS victims, set the price of the drug so high that the average patient spent $8,000 a year. Recently they have reduced the price.

10. Geraldo Rivera: The talk-show host's production company has become the leading source of air pollution in the country. He does provide temporary jobs for transvestite drug dealers and other dregs of society, though.

The Honorable J. Danforth Quayle
The White House
Washington, D.C.

Dear Mr. Vice President,

We and your fellow Americans urge you to put to rest questions about your intelligence in front of a nation-wide audience by appearing on "Jeopardy."

The future of our family and the fate of the nation require you to make this sacrifice.

Sincerely,

_____

Name

_____

Address

_____

City, State, Zip

EPILOGUE

One final story from 1989 that you may have missed: the Reverend Jerry Falwell announced that the Moral Majority would disband. That may shock you to the core, but don't worry. We at the Paragon Project are not about to let immorality run rampant in America. To take up the slack, we've vowed to intensify our efforts to ferret out immoral behavior in 1990.

And more than ever, we need your help. If you find a story or situation that you believe deserve public attention, please send the appropriate clippings to:

> The Paragon Project
> c/o St. Martin's Press
> 175 Fifth Ave.
> New York, NY 10010

Your reward will be seeing your name listed in *Scandal Annual, 1991: Who Got Caught Doing What in 1990* as an honorary investigative associate of the Paragon Project. Thanks in advance for your help.